BLACK BART

BOULEVARDIER BANDIT

by

George Hoeper

STAMP 3-13-01

D0029395

Word
Dancer
Press

Fresno, CA

RENO
DOWNTOWN
BRANCH

Copyright © 1995 by George Hoeper
All rights reserved.

Word Dancer Press
950 N. Van Ness
P.O. Box 4638
Fresno, CA 93744-4638

Printed in the United States of America

3 1235 00982 1336

Library of Congress Catalog Card Number: 94-61458

Publisher's Cataloging in Publication

Hoeper, George.
    Black Bart boulevardier bandit : the saga of California's most
mysterious stagecoach robber and the men who sought to capture him
/ George Hoeper.
    p. cm.
    Includes bibliographical references and index.
    ISBN 1-884995-05-5

    1. Black Bart, b. 1829. 2. Brigands and robbers --California--
Biography. 3. Outlaws--California--Biography. I. Title.

F866.B59H64 1994   364.1'552'092
                                    QBI94-2201

"Black Bart"

bou·le·vard·ier \bü-lə-vär-dir\ *n* : a frequenter of the boulevards; *broadly* : MAN-ABOUT-TOWN

Oregon — *Yreka*

DEL NORTE

SISKIYOU

MODOC

Eureka

HUMBOLDT

TRINITY

SHASTA

LASSEN

— *Redding*
— *Red Bluff*
— *Quincy*
— *LaPorte*
— *Downieville*
— *Oroville*
— *Nevada City*
— *Marysville*
— *Yuba City*
— *Auburn*

MENDOCINO

TEHAMA

PLUMAS

COLUSA

BUTTE

SIERRA

Ukiah

LAKE

SUTTER

YUBA

NEVADA

PLACER

Pt. Arena

SONOMA

NAPA

YOLO

SACRA-MENTO

EL DORADO

ALPINE

— *Placerville*
— *Sacramento*

Fort Ross

Duncan Mills

MARIN

SOLANO

AMADOR

— *Jackson*

CALAVERAS

Stockton

CONTRA COSTA

SAN JOAQUIN

TUOLUMNE

MONO

SAN FRANCISCO

ALAMEDA

STANISLAUS

— *Mariposa*

SAN MATEO

SANTA CLARA

MERCED

MARIPOSA

Nevada

SANTA CRUZ

SAN BENITO

FRESNO

INYO

— *Visalia*

MONTEREY

TULARE

SAN LUIS OBISPO

KERN

0 10 20 40 60 80 100 miles

SANTA BARBARA

VENTURA

LOS ANGELES

SAN BERNARDINO

SAN DIEGO

CALIFORNIA 1880

CONTENTS

Map – California 1880 iv

Preface vi

Acknowledgments vii

Map – California's Gold Country viii

Chapter 1 1

Chapter 2 18

Chapter 3 34

Chapter 4 49

Chapter 5 61

Chapter 6 74

Chapter 7 91

Chapter 8 108

Chapter 9 120

Chapter 10 131

Chapter 11 145

Appendix: Black Bart Stage Robberies 157

Notes 162

Bibliography 164

Index 166

PREFACE

Few Western outlaws with the possible exception of Jesse James, Butch Cassidy or the somewhat mythical Joaquin Murietta, stirred the public's imagination as did stage robber Black Bart, the "Po8." Unlike others whose names have become Western legend, Black Bart headed no bandit gang. Instead, for eight years he led a solitary life of outlawry, operating strictly alone. Other famous outlaws–or at least members of their gangs–left behind them a trail of innocent blood. Black Bart during his career, which involved a string of twenty-eight stage robberies, never fired a shot in anger or injured a single victim.

Most highwaymen, in robbing a stage, demanded not only its express box and sacks of U.S. Mail, but topped the deed off by robbing the passengers. One trio of bandits, after relieving a Calaveras County stage of $2,600, shamelessly demanded the stage driver hand over his watch and last five-dollar gold piece. But, not Black Bart. When, during one robbery a frightened woman leaned from the stagecoach and dropped her purse to the ground, Bart gallantly handed it back to her, stating: "It is Wells-Fargo I am robbing, not the passengers of this stage."

Clever outlaw, suave boulevardier, for nearly a decade he led Wells Fargo agents and California lawmen on a fruitless and frustrating chase. Scores of tales, true and untrue, have been told about him. This book deals with the man who called himself Black Bart, but it also tries to present a picture of the California gold country and its way of life during the latter years of the nineteenth century. And, as closely as possible, it presents the true facts surrounding the life and times of Black Bart and the people who sought to run him to ground.

Perhaps the law ultimately triumphed. At least it may have ended Bart's criminal career. But, unlike the stories of so many Western outlaws and badmen whose lives ended in a blast of gunfire, on a gallows or in prison, the Black Bart legend lives on. Where did it really end? That has become one of the enduring mysteries of the old West.

And while we may never know beyond a shadow of doubt, recent research shows Bart may have resumed his banditry after serving his prison term and subsequently died a lonely and unheralded death in the dry Nevada desert.

ACKNOWLEDGMENTS

The gathering of historical fact and information necessary for the compilation of a manuscript such as this exceeds the ability of an individual writer, within a reasonable time frame, to accomplish such an undertaking alone. Without the help and encouragement of countless others this book would not have come into print.

Special thanks must go to Calaveras County archivist and historian Lorrayne Kennedy; Amador County author and Archivist Larry Cenotto; Robert Chandler, director of Wells Fargo Bank's History Services; Charles Stone, Copperopolis native, Mother Lode historian and past president of Calaveras County Historical Society and John Boessenecker, author and Western historian.

Ron Schofield, Western artist and historian and restorer of stagecoaches and other Western rolling stock; Sharon Daniels, photographer extraordinaire; Sheryl Waller, office and museum manager, Calaveras County Historical Society; Roark Weber, whose encouragement kept this work going; Gloyd A. "Bud" Ponte and Don Cuneo, past presidents of Calaveras County Historical Society who urged that this book be written, and Howard Little, gatherer of gold country history and memorabilia.

The late Harry Webb, gatherer of Nevada and Sierra-Nevada history and teller of authentic tales; Kathy Correia, director of the California History Section of the California State Library; my wife, Alice Hoeper, a woman of infinite patience and understanding, and many others, authors, historians, publishers of periodicals whose help and information has added to the contents of this book.

G. Hoeper

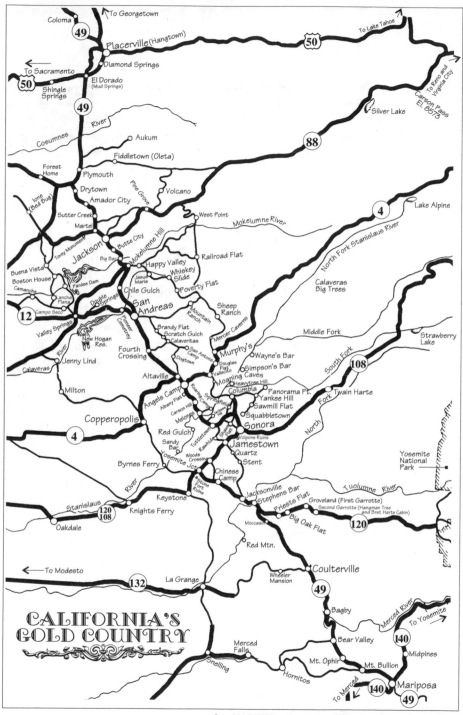

To Georgetown

Coloma

49

Placerville (Hangtown)

To Sacramento

Diamond Springs

50

El Dorado (Mud Springs)

Shingle Springs

49

Cosumnes River

Aukum

Forest Home

Fiddletown (Oleta)

Plymouth

Drytown

Ione (Bed Bug)

Amador City

Volcano

Pine Grove

Sutter Creek

Martel

West Point

Mokelumne River

Tovey Monument

Jackson

Butte City

Mokelumne Hill

Railroad Flat

Big Bar

Buena Vista

Boston House

Pardee Dam

Happy Valley

Jesus Maria

Whiskey Slide

Camanche

Lancha Plana

Double Springs

Chile Gulch

Poverty Flat

Pioneer Cemetery

12

Campo Seco

San Andreas

Mountain Ranch

Sheep Ranch

Valley Springs

New Hogan Res.

Brandy Flat

Scratch Gulch

Calaveritas

Mercer Caverns

Middle Fork

Strawberry Lake

Calaveras River

Jenny Lind

Fourth Crossing

San Antone Camp

Dogtown

Murphy's

Wayne's Bar

Calaveras Big Trees

North Fork Stanislaus River

4

Lake Alpine

Milton

Altaville

Douglas Flat

Vallecito

Simpson's Bar

Moaning Caves

South Fork

108

Angels Camp

Roaring Camp

Springfield

Heavytree Hill

Columbia

Panorama Pt.

Yankee Hill

Twain Harte

Albany Flat

Carson Hill

Cherokee

Sawmill Flat

North Fork

Copperopolis

Melones

Squabbletown

Sonora

4

Red Gulch

Tuttletown

Rawhide

Sandy Bar

Shaws Flat

Volpone Ruins

Jamestown

North

Yosemite Jct.

Woods Crossing

Quartz

Byrnes Ferry

Chinese Camp

Stent

Yosemite National Park

River

Keystone

Jacksonville

Stephens Bar

Priests Flat

Groveland (First Garrotte)

Tuolumne River

Stanislaus

120
108

Knights Ferry

Moccasin

Big Oak Flat

Second Garrotte (Hangman Tree and Bret Harte Cabin)

120

Oakdale

Red Mtn.

To Modesto

La Grange

132

Wheeler Mansion

Coulterville

49

Merced River

To Yosemite

CALIFORNIA'S GOLD COUNTRY

Bagby

Bear Valley

140

Midpines

Merced Falls

Mt. Ophir

Mt. Bullion

Snelling

Hornitos

To Merced

140

Mariposa

49

To Lake Tahoe

50

To Reno and Virginia City

Carson Pass El. 8573

Silver Lake

88

Keystone Ferry Ruins

The scent of oak leaves and dry grass mingled with the pungent smell of horse sweat and powdery red dust as the Sonora-Milton stage toiled up the steep Funk Hill grade that morning of July 26, 1875. The sun warm on his back, stage driver John Shine reclined in his seat, lines loose in his hands, and relaxed for the first time since leaving Sonora three hours earlier. The worst of the trip–the steepest and most winding–down to Reynolds Ferry in the Stanislaus River Canyon, was behind him. In another hour he would be pulling into the mining town of Copperopolis and by lunch time he would be unloading at the railroad depot in Milton.

The stage, a "mud wagon," was carrying ten passengers–eight women and children and two men–one of whom was John Olive, co-owner of the stage line[1]. As usual, it carried a U.S. mail pouch and a Wells Fargo & Company express box. But, on this occasion the box contained no gold bullion and less than three hundred dollars in gold notes. Because of the low value of the shipment, Wells Fargo had not provided the usual messenger (shotgun guard). That too was out of the ordinary, for the stagecoaches on the Sonora-Milton run, particularly on that portion lying in Calaveras County which followed the Reynolds Ferry Road, had become favorite victims of highwaymen. Stages on that run had been robbed four times in the past four years. Two of these had occurred within the past four months–on March 1 and March 23. The last netted three gunmen more then sixty-five hundred dollars[2], big money for 1875.

The stage was nearing the top of Funk Hill at the head of Yaqui Gulch, when suddenly a masked gunman brandishing a shotgun leaped from behind a boulder into the middle of the road, directly in front of the horses. As Shine struggled to control his frightened team, the bandit, his head covered by a flour sack mask, leveled the shotgun. In a firm, distinctive voice, he called out, "Please throw down the box!"

John Shine was a brave man, but he was no fool. Unarmed and looking down the wrong end of a double barreled shotgun, he had little choice but to obey the order. But, it was not easy to lift the somewhat bulky, iron bound Wells Fargo box with one hand, while holding the reins with the other. When Shine momentarily hesitated while trying to grasp the box, the gunman, still standing in the road, glanced toward the boulder strewn hillside and shouted, "If he makes a move, give him a volley, boys." From the corner of his eye as he lifted the heavy express box to toss it over the side, Shine saw what appeared to be gun barrels pointed at him from behind a rocky outcropping on the uphill side of the road.

Passenger John Olive, a young Sonora miner next to him, and several women passengers poked their heads through the stage coach windows to see what was happening. At sight of the armed man, the women withdrew from the windows with squawks of surprise and fright. From a holster at his waist the young miner whipped out a long barreled revolver, but before he could raise the gun Olive gripped his wrist and shoved the weapon toward the floor. "Put that damned thing away–do you want to get us all killed," he ordered in a loud stage whisper.

The box landed with a thump on the edge of the dusty road, and as it did, one of the now thoroughly frightened women inside the stage reached out of the window and dropped her purse on the ground. With his shotgun still aimed at the stage driver, the bandit walked forward, picked up the purse and, with a courteous bow, dropped it back into the coach.[3]

A Concord stage on the Valley Springs-Milton run, in Calaveras County. This particular road, which also served the mining town of Jenny Lind, was subject to repeated stage robberies. Stage driver Reason McConnell was held up twice by bandits while driving this route.

"I don't want your money–only the express box and mail." Then, with a sweep of his hand, he motioned John Shine to drive on up the hill. Shine, as he pulled away, chanced a glance backward and saw the bandit already attacking the express box with a hatchet.

Shine's stage had hardly disappeared up the grade when a second stagecoach, driven by Donald McLean of Sonora, rounded a curve and came upon the masked man still laboring with the hatchet to open the express box. An instant later McLean and his several passengers found themselves confronted by the business end of the shotgun.

"Please throw down the box," the masked gunman requested, but the stage was allowed to pass undisturbed after McLean informed the bandit he was carrying no treasure. The road agent made no attempt to rob McLean or his passengers of their personal funds.

At the top of the hill McLean's stage caught up with Shine's, and there both halted while the drivers, accompanied by several

3

male passengers, walked back to where they could view the robbery scene. As they drew close enough to clearly see the boulder behind which the robber had been hiding, they were shocked to find the rifle barrels they had seen pointing at them were nothing more than sticks which had been carefully arranged to look like guns.

With the empty express box and the mail sacks the bandit had cut open, Shine hurriedly completed the trip to Copperopolis, where he reported the robbery to Wells Fargo agent J. M. Pike. Pike immediately sent a telegram to San Andreas, the county seat, to notify Calaveras County Sheriff Benjamin Thorn, while Shine continued his trip to Milton.[4]

In relating details of the robbery to the Copperopolis Wells Fargo agent, and on the following day to Sheriff Thorn, several things stood out in John Shine's memory. The stage robber wore a unique mask–a flour sack with eyeholes cut in it, that covered his entire head and hat. He wore a soiled linen duster over what appeared to be rough, miner's clothing, and his boots were covered by heavy woolen boot socks, apparently to distort his foot prints.

But, the one thing that most sharply had impressed itself in the stage driver's mind was the bandit's politeness. "Please throw down the box . . ." It would be this stage robber's surprising courtesy, along with the flour sack mask, the soiled duster and something Sheriff Thorn was to make a note of the next day–the "T" shaped slash in the heavy canvas mail sack–that were to become trademarks of this man who later was to become known as Black Bart.

Sheriff Thorn reached the robbery scene that afternoon but found little to provide him, or Wells Fargo Chief of Detectives James B. Hume, with any solid clues. They found a trampled spot behind a large boulder on the hillside above the road, where the gunman had apparently waited in concealment for arrival of the stage. In the road they found his boot tracks and where he had kneeled in the dust to smash the express box with the hatchet. Behind the rock over which the bandit had arranged sticks to look like gun barrels, Thorn found a real 12-gauge shotgun buried in the leaves.

Whether the gun was a second one which the bandit, for

some reason, had brought to the robbery scene or was the gun he had used in the holdup, then buried, they did not know. Some of the passengers who had been on the stage and had seen the robber said that in addition to the shotgun which he pointed at the stage driver, he also carried a Henry rifle slung over his shoulder on a strap. If he was carrying a rifle, it was one of the few times during his eight-year robbery career that he was armed with anything except a shotgun.[5]

Thorn and Hume noted that the shotgun, unloaded but in good working condition, was a breech loading side hammer 12-gauge, with its twin barrels shortened to something less than twenty-four inches. At close range, a gun of that type loaded with buckshot would throw a formidable pattern. The officers surmised that the bandit, if also armed with a repeating rifle, chose to leave the shotgun behind rather than be encumbered by a second weapon during his flight through the mountainous terrain.

Except for the shotgun, they came away from the robbery site with no more clues or useful information on the holdup than they had arrived with. Nevertheless, within the week Wells Fargo circulated a poster, dated July 27, 1875 listing details of the robbery. The reward offered was for more than the amount the company reported losing to the gunman. How much the bandit may have found in the mail sacks was never ascertained. The poster, as issued by Wells Fargo, stated: "REWARD! Wells Fargo & Company's express box containing $160 in gold notes, was robbed this morning, by one man, on the route from Sonora to Milton, near the top of the hill between the river and Copperopolis. $250 and one-fourth of any money recovered, will be paid for the arrest and conviction of the robber." The flyer was posted throughout the Mother Lode, but it did not result in the gathering of enough information to pay for the ink used to print it. This uniquely polite bandit, who was to chalk up a string of at least twenty-eight stage robberies over a period of eight years, remained an enigma to lawmen. Even though the men who hunted him quickly became familiar with his distinct method of operation, they had no name at all to place on him until after his fourth successful robbery.

Following the July 26 Sonora-Milton robbery, this bandit simply dropped out of sight. Because no one had seen his face, there was no way of tracing or identifying him. He was not heard of again until almost the end of the year. Then, on the cold wintry morning of December 28, in the digger pine and scrub oak covered foothills a few miles north of Smartsville, in Nevada County, the flour sack masked bandit, shotgun in hand, halted the North San Juan-Marysville stage driven by Mike Hogan. It was the second time in two weeks that Hogan's stage had been robbed on this run. Angered by his ill luck, Hogan nevertheless prudently complied when the gunman, motioning at him with the gaping, twin shotgun barrels, politely instructed him in a deep, authoritative voice to toss down the mail sacks and Wells Fargo box. Hogan and an unidentified passenger later said they thought a second man was involved because they saw a gunbarrel protruding from behind a log at the edge of the road. What they probably observed, said Wells Fargo Detective Chief James Hume, was a stick arranged to look like a gun–the same ruse used by the bandit during the July 26 robbery on Funk Hill.

Hogan hurried his team to Marysville, gathered a posse and was back at the robbery scene in less than four hours, but except for the smashed express box, which, according to the Marysville newspaper, had yielded only a few hundred dollars, they could pick up no trace of the stage robber or clues to his identity. The mail sacks, which had contained an undetermined amount, had been slashed from top to bottom to form an inverted "T." A unique slit that was to become very well known to Jim Hume over the ensuing years.

Apparently the bandit had fled the robbery scene on foot. Rain, which began falling later in the day, aided his escape by washing out his tracks. "This job," said Hume in grudging admiration, "is the work of a professional."[6]

More than six months elapsed before the flour-sack masked bandit struck again. Then on the night of June 2, 1876, some five miles north of Cottonwood, about four miles below the Oregon-California state line, he robbed the Roseburg, Oregon-Yreka stage of express box and mail pouch. His tactics were generally the same, but this robbery also marked the start of the bandit's use of darkness to help shield his operations. In fact, Black Bart was one of the few highwaymen who committed stage robberies at night.

On this moonlit night stage driver A. C. Adams' six-horse

6

At this spot, near the top of Funk Hill, in the Stanislaus River Canyon, Black Bart committed his first and last stage robberies. He hid behind the large rock on the left and placed sticks across the top of it to stimulate gun barrels.

team was traveling slowly up a steep rise when, from the shadows, a man stepped in front of the horses and ordered Adams to stop. Aided by the moonlight and the dim glow of his stage lamps, Adams could see that the man was holding a gun and was wearing what appeared to be a sack over his head. Exhibiting his usual firm courtesy, the masked man demanded the express box and mail pouches. When Adams hesitated, the bandit raised his gun threateningly. The entire episode lasted only minutes. Although there were several passengers aboard the stage, no effort was made to rob them.

When he finally arrived in Cottonwood, Adams reported the robbery, but because of darkness, pursuit could not be undertaken until morning. At daybreak, a passerby found the smashed express box lying beside the road where the robbery took place. Again, the mail sacks had been opened with the now too familiar slit. Deputy Sheriff John Halleck arrived later in the morning to take up the stage robber's trail, but other than some boot tracks

7

in the road, he found no clues. The tracks pointed east toward a promontory in the Siskiyou Mountains the locals called Pilot Rock. Pilot Rock was used as a landmark by early travelers between Roseburg and Yreka when the route was only a dimly marked trail. Now the earth was dry and hard, making the tracking difficult, and before the day was out the trail was lost.

James Hume arrived from San Francisco, made inquiries and announced that his company was offering $250 for information leading to the arrest and conviction of the stage robber. The State of California shortly thereafter sweetened the reward pot with another $300. The offers brought forth no information. And, as now was becoming more common, Wells Fargo officials declined to disclose their company's loss. Many felt that to admit a large take by bandits in any single holdup would only encourage other outlaws to try their luck at Wells Fargo's expense. In fact, it was the practice of James Hume and Wells Fargo General Superintendent John J. Valentine to play down their company's losses to banditry. Quite possibly, the flour sack masked bandit's take in the Roseburg-Yreka robbery was substantial, for that was his only known activity for the year 1876. In fact, it was more than a year before he struck again.

If the man who was soon to become known as Black Bart did not overwork himself in the stage robbery business that year, there were plenty of others who kept the trade flourishing. In fact, stage robbery became so prevalent in the Redding-Yreka area that by year's end some local citizens were suggesting federal protection.

The editor of the Yreka Union wrote the following comment: "We learn the Shasta and Redding Stage was stopped on Thursday morning near Shasta by highwaymen and compelled to give up the Wells Fargo Company's express. As on the stoppage on Monday, they got nothing but letters as far as is now known. This makes the third time within a week that highwaymen have stopped the stage within Shasta County and the fourth time within two weeks. This is getting somewhat monotonous for the people of Shasta County and we expect to hear about the next thing, that some highwaymen have been seriously hurt. The $600 reward for the arrest and conviction of each and every highwayman within the state ought to be some inducement.

"If the robberies of the mail and express between Yreka and

Redding continue, Wells Fargo & Company may draw off the route, as it is a losing business to them, having barely made expenses last year and liable to lose money this year if more raids are made upon the treasure box. . . . If the mail is continually molested every trip the contractors might call on the military authorities for a cavalry escort which the government is bound to furnish."

The idea of cavalry-escorted stages never even became a serious suggestion. Least worried of all concerning use of troopers to protect the stages appeared to be the bandits, who continued to strike sporadically along the stage routes. If the flour sack bandit was conspicuous by his absence from the field of stage robbery during those months, it is doubtful it was caused by the threat of federal cavalry intervention.

The Redding-Yreka robberies finally tapered off as some of the criminal element ran afoul of the law, and others, possibly seeking more lucrative fields, moved on.

On August 3, 1877, the flour sack masked bandit robbed a stage near the Russian River on the Point Arena-Duncan Mills run, and from that day, he was no longer nameless. From the express box the bandit took three hundred dollars in coin and a check for $302.52, written on the Grangers Bank of San Francisco, that was never cashed.

The stage, driven by Ash Wilkinson, left Point Arena at 6:00 a.m. with seven passengers for the fifty-five-mile trip to Duncan Mills. It was not a journey to be awaited with anticipation. The stage was a light, bone jarring mud wagon that left its passengers pretty much exposed to the elements. They could not expect, even with good luck, to arrive at the lumber town of Duncan Mills much before 7:00 p.m. that evening. At mid-morning the stage left the coast, climbed into the mountains past the settlement of Plantation, then turned south again to change horses and have lunch at Henry's Hotel on the Russian River near where State Highway 128 now exists. Mid-afternoon found them topping Meyers Grade, several miles south of abandoned Fort Ross, southernmost point of penetration by Russian traders along the California coast.

Passengers, stage driver and horses were looking forward to the end of the day's long journey when a few turns from the top of the ridge a flour sack masked man pointed a shotgun at Wilkinson and told him to stop. As in past robberies the gunman wore a soiled duster over what appeared to be laborer's clothing. He demanded the Wells-Fargo box and the mail bags and made no attempt to rob the driver or passengers. As box and mail bags fell from the stage, the gunman motioned the driver to move on.

But, what proved most startling and intriguing to lawmen and to newsmen, who immediately made the most of it, was the note he left behind, weighted down by a rock atop a roadside stump. On the back of a waybill he had taken from the Wells Fargo express box, the stage robber had boldly scribbled:

I've labored long for bread
For honor and for riches,
But on my corns too long you've tread
You fine haired Sons of Bitches.

The missive was signed "Black Bart, the Po8."

Below the four-line stanza Bart had penned a postscript: "Driver, give my respects to our old friend, the other driver. I really had a notion to hang my old disguise hat on his weather eye."

Each line of the poem and message to the driver had been penned in a different hand, apparently in an attempt to disguise the bandit's true handwriting.[7]

Now Wells Fargo's chief of detectives working from his San Francisco office, had a name for this wide ranging stage robber, but he still had little else. To Jim Hume the situation was frustrating. No one had seen the man's face. He carried a shotgun with which he threatened stage drivers and intimidated passengers, but which he never fired. He apparently traveled cross-country, camping out most of the time, and he traveled on foot, so there was no chance of tracing or identifying him through use of a rental horse or buggy. He apparently preferred the silence of the woods and was well aware that the appearance of a stranger in a backwoods settlement or some crossroads store stirred curiosity and questions. He knew the best way to remain anonymous was simply to remain unseen.

Hume sent confidential letters to his company's agents

throughout the north state and to all sheriffs and constables, seeking information on any suspicious persons they might have seen or heard about, moving through their local areas. As in the past, his efforts bore no fruit.

The man now known as Black Bart did not rob again in 1877 and, in fact, remained inactive until the summer of 1878. Then, on July 25, just a mile beyond Berry Creek Sawmill, in addition to relieving the Quincy-Oroville stage of Wells Fargo & Company's express box and the pouch containing the U.S. Mail, the Po8 again exercised his literary skills. This time, he left the following eight-line verse:

> *Here I lay me down to sleep,*
> *To wait the coming morrow.*
> *Perhaps success, perhaps defeat,*
> *And everlasting sorrow.*
> *Let come what will I'll try it on,*
> *My condition can't be worse;*
> *And if there's money in that box*
> *Tis munny in my purse.*
> *Black Bart, the Po8.*

There were no other deliberate clues found at the robbery scene, but Jim Hume surmised that this bandit was becoming bolder. This time a man had been seen the day before, sitting beside the road at almost the same spot where the robbery occurred. The Wells Fargo detective and local law enforcement men believed it probably was the bandit, checking the time the stage would arrive at that point.

They also determined that the stage robber was no longer taking the precaution of wearing socks or rags wrapped around his boots to hide his footprints. At the robbery scene they found in the dust clear prints of what appeared to be a size six or eight boot.

The eight lines of doggerel were the last the Po8 would ever leave at a robbery scene, even though he would commit at least twenty-three more stage robberies over the next five and a half years.

Taken by the bandit from the express box was $379 in coins–

considerably more than the "little or nothing" Wells Fargo officers told anxious newspaper reporters. Wells Fargo's claim of only a minor loss appears to be just another indication that the company made a habit of misleading the public about its losses to bandits in order to discourage potential outlaws. Also taken in the Quincy-Oroville robbery was a twenty-five-dollar silver watch and a two hundred-dollar diamond ring which Bart reportedly kept and wore regularly. How much was taken from the U.S. Mail sacks remains unknown.

The year of 1878 proved a busy one for Black Bart. In addition to the Quincy-Oroville holdup, just five days later, on July 30, he robbed the LaPorte stage. There, he continued his courteous ways, requesting the driver to "please throw down the box!" And in removing the mail from its canvas sacks, he continued unknowingly to leave his trademark, the "T" shaped slashes in the mail bags. Observing the T shaped slash, a Wells Fargo agent said, "He might just as well have signed his name."

If the Wells Fargo robbery report is to be believed, his effort garnered only fifty dollars in gold nuggets and another watch. Stage driver Dan Barry said that shortly after sunup, about six miles west of LaPorte, a man wearing a duster and a sack with eye holes cut in it stepped from the heavily timbered roadside in the path of the stage and leveled a shotgun at him. As clouds of dust welled up from the wagon wheels and the milling horses' hooves, Barry pulled his team to a halt. As per the gunman's instructions, the driver tossed out mail sacks and the express box without protest. With a wave of his hand, the gunman motioned Barry to go on. Hardly two minutes had elapsed between the time that Black Bart stepped from the sheltering trees and the time the stage was once more on its way, minus express box and mail sacks.

A Plumas County posse dispatched by Sheriff James H. Yeates found no poetry and, except for tracks in the dust made by about a size eight boot, no clues.

Bart was not heard of again for three months. Then, on October 2, and again on October 3, 1878 he pulled off bold robberies, the second of which came close to being his undoing. On the afternoon of October 2, about ten miles north of Ukiah at a spot ever after known as "Robber's Rock" or "Black Bart Rock," the flour sack hooded gunman stopped the Arcata-Ukiah stage. Shielded by a huge boulder that stood at the road's edge, the bandit pointed his shotgun at stage driver Alex Fowler and ordered him to halt. Fowler, who was not accompanied by an armed guard, reportedly was carrying a sawed-off shotgun himself. However, he was given no chance to pull it from the scabbard where it rode beside him, and wisely, he gave up the express box and sacks of mail.

A "mud wagon," typical of the light four-horse stages commonly used in California's Mother Lode foothills to transport passengers, mail and Wells Fargo & Company express boxes. The mud wagons cost less, were easier to pull and did not bog down as easily on muddy roads as did the heavier Concord stages built in the East.

Again, the Wells Fargo loss was said to be trifling. The company claimed the express box contained only forty dollars and a gold watch. At least, with three watches collected during recent robberies, Bart was going to be able to tell time.

First arrivals at the robbery scene found a trampled spot beside the rock and a number of apple cores, indicating the bandit had waited a considerable time for arrival of the stage. Mendocino County Sheriff James R. Moore arrived from Ukiah, the county seat, but found little except the apple cores and the mail sacks with the "T" shaped slashes. He returned from that robbery scene the next day only to find that a few hours earlier the Covelo-Ukiah stage had been robbed near Centerville, on the Potter Valley Road. And, although the two robberies had been committed more than twenty miles from each other and something less than sixteen hours apart, it appeared from descriptions given by passengers and stage drivers that both holdups were the work of the same man. The amount taken in the second robbery was estimated at something in excess of four hundred dollars, but an exact figure was difficult to determine because the stage had taken on shipments at several small way stations. The bandit did not rob stage driver Nathan Waltrip or his passengers.

Slits in the mail sacks told the sheriff that the man known as Black Bart had probably committed the October 3 robbery. Several fresh peach pits found beside the road where the bandit stood indicated that he had breakfasted on fruit picked along the way. Sheriff Moore, an accomplished woodsman and tracker, took the bandit's trail, which headed eastward, toward Bartlet Springs and Lake County. For the remainder of that day and throughout the next, Moore, riding horseback but many times dismounting to pick up his quarry's dim track, felt he still had a good chance to catch the fleeing stage robber. Finally, around midday on October 5, after tracking his man nearly sixty miles, Moore gave up when the trail petered out in the grasslands at the edge of the foothills, some ten miles west of the town of Williams. What also troubled Moore was that he doubted a man on foot could cover that much rough country in so short a time. He worried that somewhere along the way he had lost the bandit's track and was following some innocent person whose trail had crossed Black Bart's.

Meanwhile, as Wells Fargo General Manager John Valentine fumed and James Hume, with increasing frustration, combed his files of known criminals for clues, a man called Charles Bolton was enjoying the good life in San Francisco. This suave, well groomed gentleman, known to friends as a successful Mother Lode mine owner and mining engineer, was seen only in the better places with people of good standing. Always correctly attired, he enjoyed the theater, the city's better music halls and fine restaurants. Over the years he had gained a wide circle of friends and acquaintances, including city and police officials. He had become a welcome guest in many of San Francisco's better homes. Although he is not known to have forged any serious or lasting female relationships, he was observed on occasion escorting any one of the several quite acceptable and eligible matrons whose husbands had passed on.

14

From his quarters in the Webb House, a well kept hotel in the Webb Building at 37 Post Street, Bolton ventured forth to enjoy a life of leisure in what was then the West Coast's most prestigious city. He was not a drinking man, and one of his few indulgences was the occasional placing of bets on horse races or prize fights.

From time to time he would disappear, sometimes for a few days, sometimes for a few weeks. His friends believed he was up in the Mother Lode inspecting his mining operations or involved in a mining engineering project for some client. Upon his return he might speak briefly on his mining situation or about mining in general in the gold country. As to his own mine holdings, he always remained sufficiently vague to discourage any detailed discussion. People generally construed this reticence to talk about his own mining ventures simply as a reluctance to give away information about a good thing. Because he was known as a successful mine owner and mining expert, he occasionally was sought out by friends of friends who sought advice on mining stocks or investments. He usually attempted to sidestep those inquiries and gambits for advice, but when pressed, he had a convincing enough store of knowledge and information concerning geology, mining methods and lore to pass himself off as an expert.

Intelligent, an interesting conversationalist, obviously a man of means who frequented the city's best watering holes, he undoubtedly had at least a nodding acquaintance with such nabobs as Leland Stanford, Lloyd Tevis, James Flood, John Mackay, Adolph Sutro, Lucky Baldwin and James Fair. It is doubtful, however, that he attempted any close association with the mining magnates, lest he be questioned too closely about his own mining interests and background.

Few persons who knew him could imagine polite, well groomed Charles Bolton as anything other than what he said he was. No one in his circle of friends seemed to notice that his absences from the city coincided with some of the mountain area's stage robberies.

In fact, in bustling, cosmopolitan San Francisco, stage robberies in the hills caused little stir except in the Montgomery Street office of Wells Fargo & Company. Even the doggerel left behind by the bold bandit who signed his work "Black Bart, the Po8," drew only the temporary interest of San Franciscans. Certainly, they had no reason to suspect that one of their own–least of all this suave mine owner-engineer–could in any way be connected to such a base profession as stage robbery. Not for years would they learn that the stage robber who called himself Black Bart was none other than the respected man they knew as Charles E. Bolton, whose real name was Charles Boles.

As Black Bart, this enigmatic man took on a totally opposite character from that of the citified gentleman known to his fellow San Franciscans. Although he preferred and thoroughly enjoyed the amenities of city life, Black Bart was tough of body and mind, and able to withstand the most severe rigors of the outdoors. With the tools of his trade, the shotgun, axe or crowbar for opening express boxes, a bit of food and a change of clothes wrapped in a single blanket, he traveled the back country, avoiding the more well-used roads or trails. Thoroughly woodswise, he faced any kind of weather and covered great distances through wilderness or over mountain trails in the space of a few short hours. Soon after committing a stage holdup he would be miles away, as always, using his legs to outdistance the lawmen who were trailing him. His ability to move so swiftly on foot constantly confounded pursuing lawmen. The prime example is his flight from Mendocino County sheriff James Moore who, close on Bart's heels, turned back, at least partially, because he doubted any individual could have traveled such a distance in so short a period of time.

Often Bart's robberies occurred so many miles apart and within such a short time span that most lawmen, including Wells Fargo special agents, thought they were being committed by two or more men who had adopted the flour sack disguise.

Although the amounts he obtained from its treasure boxes were not large, Black Bart was becoming a very sharp thorn in Wells Fargo's side. Jim Hume's frustrations with this elusive highwayman were growing by the day. The price on Bart's head also was growing. Wells Fargo raised the ante from $250 to $300, and this amount was matched by the State of California–an almost unprecedented act on the part of that governmental entity. The U.S. Post Office Department added another $200 to bring the reward for his capture and conviction to a total of $800. In that day and age, that amount of money was an enticing lure, but it brought no results.

One factor weighing heavily in favor of Black Bart was that he had no prior criminal record through which he could be identified as a possible suspect. Although this bandit now had a name, or at least a pseudonym, the law still did not know who he was or very much about him. He left law enforcement officials and Wells Fargo agents groping in the dark.

But their dearth of information did not keep local sheriffs or James Hume from speculating.[8] Following the Black Bart robberies of 1877 and 1878, Hume convinced himself that the elusive bandit was the one-eyed Frank Fox, former stage robber who, after serving his several years in San Quentin Prison, had been paroled. Following the Ukiah stage robberies in October, the Wells Fargo detective chief mailed a confidential notice to police, sheriff's departments and Wells Fargo agents throughout northern and central California, listing the Po8 robbery suspect as Frank Fox. He described Fox and stated, "From information in my possession, I am satisfied that one Frank Fox committed the following robberies, at two of which he left at the scene, some doggerel signed, Black Bart. Please arrest the said Frank Fox and telegraph the undersigned or the Sheriff of Mendocino County. Any old convict who served time in San Quentin when Fox was there, will know him."

But, unknown to Hume, Fox, by that time, had left California, presumably for the Middle West where he was from originally. At least, he was not arrested and Hume was spared the embarrassment of having fingered the wrong man.[9]

Somewhere, either from a Wells Fargo express box or one of the mail pouches he opened, Black Bart must have taken a sizable sum during the final months of 1878, for he did not rob another stage until June 21, 1879. Then, for the second time in his career, Bart hit the LaPorte-Oroville stage owned by Dr. S. T. Brewster. Three miles west of Forbestown, Bart stepped from roadside bushes into the path of the horses. With shotgun pointed at driver Dave Quadlin's chest, he demanded the Wells Fargo treasure box and mail sacks. Without an armed messenger, there was little Quadlin could do but comply.

Wells Fargo's LaPorte agent, Sam Wheeler, said when the stagecoach left his office that morning its express box contained only fifty dollars and a silver watch. Since the amount was small, Wheeler's statement probably was true. Had the express box held a large amount, Wheeler probably would have followed company policy and refused to name a specific figure. What Bart found in the U.S. Mail sacks is unknown. At any rate, he slipped away from the LaPorte stage robbery scene undetected, despite a serious effort by Plumas County Sheriff James H. Yeates to track him down. He was not heard of again until October 25, when he robbed the Roseburg, Oregon-Redding stage.

The Oregon-bound stage left Redding an hour before sundown on October 25, traveling fast to take advantage of the remaining daylight. Then, with darkness falling and his coach lamps lighted, driver James Smithson was allowing his horses to slow down as they climbed Bass Hill, near the settlement of Buckeye, when a masked gunman stepped from the shadows and forced him to halt.

Ordered to "throw down the box," Smithson replied that he could not. The express box, he told the bandit, was chained down inside the stagecoach. Then, appearing not to be particularly rattled by that disclosure, the masked man ordered Smithson down off the driver's box and to walk forward and hold the lead horses' bridles. The man, who from his dress Smithson recognized as the well publicized Black Bart, instructed the stage's only passenger, Mrs. Hattie Bigelow, out of the vehicle and to stand some distance away, while, with an axe, he went to work on the express box.

Opening of the box took longer than Bart had anticipated and while hammering away at it he exhibited considerable frustration. Finally the strong box gave way to his efforts. Then without waiting for the stage to leave, he pulled out a knife and cut open the canvas mail sacks. Only after extracting the registered letters did he tell the driver and passenger to get back on the stage and move on. Supposedly, the express box contained only a small shipment of valuables, but the registered letters, according to local newspapers, yielded at least a thousand dollars. The opened letters were found the next day in a nearby ravine.

Two days later, on October 27, 1879, and some twenty miles cross-country from the Bass Hill holdup, Black Bart robbed the Redding-Alturas stage. The robbery occurred about twenty-five miles east of Redding, between Millville and the settlement of Round Mountain. Stage driver Ed Payne was easing his four-horse team and mud wagon along a particularly narrow, winding stretch of road when Bart made his appearance.

As he rounded a turn, Payne found the flour-sack masked man armed with a shotgun, standing in the middle of the road. He did not need to be told to stop. There was nothing else to do but bring his stage to a halt, and he did not argue when the bandit told him to throw down the Wells Fargo box and mail pouches.

As soon as box and bags hit the dust of the boulder strewn road, the gunman ordered Payne to move on and cautioned him not to look back.

Upon reaching Millville shortly before dark, Payne reported the robbery, and three lawmen, one of them a U.S. Postal detective, prepared to ride to the robbery scene. They were there when daylight came and took up Bart's trail, which headed south, but he followed a route through rough, unpopulated country, and they soon lost it.

Reportedly, the express box opened at the October 27 robbery scene gave up only a small amount of money or valuables, but the papers again claimed that he realized as much as thirteen hundred dollars from the mail.

It appeared that Bart preferred to confine his activities to the less densely populated outlying counties even though the express boxes on their stages generally contained less value than those on heavily guarded coaches in the Mother Lode. It was his company's trifling losses in the LaPorte and two Shasta County robberies that prompted Wells Fargo detective boss Jim Hume to comment that "stage robbers would do well to take only the U.S. Mail sacks and leave Wells Fargo's express boxes alone. The postal authorities almost never make more than a token effort to apprehend bandits, while we at Wells Fargo expend every effort to put them behind bars."

What Hume said, at least to some extent, was true. Concerning robbery and theft, the company's motto was, "Wells Fargo: We Never Forget!" The company's agents would work as hard to catch a highwayman who had committed a fifty-dollar robbery as they would to capture a man who had robbed an express box of five thousand dollars. On more than one occasion they followed men halfway across the continent to arrest them, and in at least one instance, followed an embezzler to the South Seas.

In addition to robberies, during its early years, the company suffered heavily from internal thefts. In 1852, a Stockton Wells Fargo agent made off with $70,000, and clerks in Mariposa and Mokelumne Hill took $40,000 and $50,000 respectively.[1] During the 1870's a relief clerk in Wells Fargo's Auburn office disappeared after making off with the contents of the office safe including a twenty-pound chunk of quartz rock laced with gold.

And there were other robberies of course, some preceding Black Bart by nearly a quarter of a century. As the gold country's population increased, bringing with it more than a fair share of undesirables, stage holdups increased on a proportionate scale. What was possibly the Sierra Nevada foothills' first stage robbery occurred in April, 1852, even before the opening of the first Wells Fargo office in California. Self styled badman Reelfoot Williams and several accomplices held up a stage near Illinoistown (present day Colfax on Interstate 80) and took $7,000 in gold bullion. A hurriedly-formed posse caught up with the bandits a short time later, near the Yuba River. A brief gun battle ensued and the Reelfoot Williams gang was permanently out of business.[2]

On September 5, 1853, an Adams Company stage leaving Sonora lost $25,000 to bandits less than a mile out of town. A $10,000 reward was offered, but there is no record of the robbers ever being caught.

Early-day robbery gang leader Tom Bell, whose real name was Dr. Thomas J. Hodges, fled through Calaveras County in 1856 after his gang bungled an August 11 holdup of the Camptonville-Marysville stage which reputedly was carrying $100,000 in raw gold. Instead of "throwing down the box," the Wells Fargo messenger guarding the gold shipment opened fire. He killed one of Bell's men, but a woman passenger on the stage was hit by one of the bandit gang's bullets. Bell fled to the southern mines and was hiding at a friend's ranch near Knight's Ferry, on the Stanislaus River, when a posse closed in on him some weeks later. Bell confessed to the attempted robbery and slaying and was hanged on the spot.[3]

During the early years of the gold rush, stage robberies such as those were the exception rather than the rule. And, more often than not, those who committed them were quickly brought to justice.

Notable among the Mother Lode's early day badmen was Richard Barter, "Rattlesnake Dick," the high point of whose relatively short career involved the hijacking in 1855 of a gold-laden mule train traveling from Weaverville to Red Bluff. Within weeks after the gold theft most of Barter's gang was headed for San Quentin Prison, and in 1857 Barter was killed in a running gunfight with a sheriff's posse near Auburn.

Another example of quick justice that discouraged highwaymen during the earlier gold rush years occurred when shortly after daybreak on February 17, 1857, three men robbed the Murphys-Stockton stage of $27,000 in Calaveras County, about a mile south of Murphys. The stage actually was carrying $32,000 in gold, $5,000 of which was in a box owned by the Pacific Express Company. The remainder was in a Wells Fargo express box. In their haste, the gunmen did not bother to open the Pacific Express box, and in smashing open the Wells Fargo box, left $1,300 scattered on the ground.

The bandits left the robbery scene on foot. Mud from the rain which had fallen during the night made it easy for possemen from Murphys and nearby Vallecito to track them. The tracks led to a cabin on Coyote Creek, little more than a mile from where the robbery occurred. By noon, unsuccessful miners David Waldin, Barry Browning and a man named Langley had been taken into custody. Meanwhile, other members of the posse found the $27,000 where the robbers had buried it only a few hundred yards from the holdup scene. A few days later all three men pleaded guilty to the robbery. Waldin was sentenced to twelve years in prison; Browning to eight. Langley received only a four-year sentence because he had been the most cooperative with his captors.

In 1875, the year that Black Bart began his operations, stages in northern and central California were the victims of thirty-four robberies and attempted robberies. Five of the holdups occurred in Calaveras County. On March 1, Mitchell Brown, alias "Little Mitch," in company with Mitchell Ratovich, "Big Mitch," robbed the Mokelumne Hill-Lodi stage.

On March 23 the same two bandits, in company with Ramon Ruiz and Antone Savage, "Old Joaquin," robbed the Milton-Sonora stage of $6,500. On July 26, Black Bart entered the stage robbery picture with his classic heist of the Sonora-Milton stage, and on October 23, Big and Little Mitch with Ruiz and Old Joaquin, again hit the Sonora-Milton stage. Closing the stage robbery activity in Calaveras County for 1875, bandits held up the Chinese Camp-Copperopolis stage on December 6. Total robbery losses in California in 1875 cost Wells Fargo & Company $80,000, an important amount of money for that era.

Between 1870 and 1884, Wells Fargo Detective Chief James Hume recorded 313 stage robberies and thirty-four attempted robberies involving Wells Fargo treasure shipments. During those years, according to Hume, the company's robbery losses totaled approximately $405,000. Stage robberies, rare during the 1850's, continued to increase, but it was not until the mid-60's that they began to present a real security problem for Wells Fargo. Then, during the years Black Bart was chalking up his string of robberies, stage robbery hit its peak.

On January 8, 1881, Wells Fargo's General Superintendent J. J. Valentine distributed the following circular: "Due to losses that have become too frequent and onerous, we yesterday ordered discontinuance of service from Auburn to Greenwood, Georgetown, Todds Valley, Foresthill and Michigan Bluff. We will probably be compelled to take similar action in other areas."[4]

Sam Dorsey, agent in charge of Wells Fargo's Grass Valley office, is said during the early 60's to have initiated the practice of hiring guards to protect shipments of gold and other valuables on the Grass Valley-Colfax run. His idea was quickly adopted by other agents, and by the end of 1861 the company had 16 shotgun messengers in its employ. By 1870 there were thirty-five shotgun guards working for Wells Fargo, and by 1880 the number had increased to 200 and was still growing. But, even at the height of its stage robbery losses, not all stages carried Wells Fargo guards.

Even after stage service reached virtually all areas of the Mother Lode and the West, not all gold shipments traveled by Wells Fargo express. Some major gold producers, particularly the owners of large hydraulic mines who were washing great volumes of gold from ancient river channels, continued to protect their own bullion shipments between mine and rail head. The mine owners placed their gold shipments aboard wagons on which at least two guards rode with the driver. Preceding the wagon some fifty or seventy-five yards would be a pair of mounted men armed with rifles. Following the wagon at a discreet distance would be two more guards armed with Winchesters or shotguns. Those hard-eyed men, all of whom were dead shots, took all the profit out of highway robbery. On one occasion, it was noted in the newspaper, a wagon left the Amador County mining camp of Volcano

23

REWARD

WELLS, FARGO & CO.'S EXPRESS BOX

on **SONORA AND MILTON STAGE ROUTE**, was **ROBBED** this morning, near Reynolds' Ferry, by one man, masked and armed with sixteen shooter and double-barreled shot gun. We will pay

$250

for **ARREST** and **CONVICTION** of the Robber.

JNO. J. VALENTINE, Gen. Supt

Wells Fargo began circulation of this poster on July 27, 1875, the day after Black Bart robbed the Sonora-Milton Stage on Funk Hill, in Calaveras County

with $150,000 in gold, accompanied by nine armed men, most of them owners of the greater part of the shipment.

Nevertheless, Wells Fargo express boxes carried the vast majority of the Mother Lode's gold shipments, and it also employed tough, dedicated shotgun messengers. Those men, such as Mike Tovey, Aaron Ross, Eugene Blair and Fred Jackson, all at one time or another stood off attempted stage robberies and all had "fetched their man." They were noted for shooting first and asking questions afterward. It was lucky for Black Bart, who boasted of committing all of his robberies with an unloaded gun, that he never attempted the robbery of a stage on which one of those men was riding shotgun.

In addition to the losses of express box contents taken as the result of shotgun levied liens, there were other equally high costs connected with the robberies. Hume, in an 1885 crime report, listed $73,451 paid out in rewards for information leading to the arrests and convictions of criminals. Another $22,307 went to attorneys who assisted in the prosecution of bandits and burglars. He set incidental costs connected with crime suppression at

24

$90,070. Salaries for guards and special officers cost the company $326,517, for a total during that fourteen-year period of $917,411.

Stagecoach robbery had become such a common occurrence by 1882 that Wells Fargo had adopted a printed form for its employees to fill out when reporting stage robberies. But, Wells Fargo shotgun guards and detectives took pains to ensure that stage robbery became neither a particularly healthful or profitable business. During that fourteen years on which Hume reported, five stagecoach bandits were killed and more than twice that many, including Black Bart, were wounded. Seven robbery suspects were hanged by angry citizens–mostly in Nevada and Arizona–and 206 stage robbers were convicted and sent to prison.

Wells Fargo casualties during that same period included four stage drivers killed, four seriously wounded, two guards killed and four wounded. In addition, four passengers were killed.

To novice badmen, the network of stages traveling remote foothill and mountain roads, virtually all carrying treasure, must have seemed like easy pickings. They soon learned, however, that robbing a stage was much like poking a stick into a hornet's nest. Most were quickly tracked down and arrested. And, although Black Bart and his kind continued to rifle its express boxes, Wells Fargo customers whose shipments fell into the hands of bandits never lost a dime. The company had a policy of making good, immediately, on any robbery loss suffered by the people who utilized its express box services. As an example, when bandits robbed a stage and took $8,300 which was being shipped from Iowa Hill to Sacramento, Wells Fargo paid the Sacramento banking company of T. S. Fiske the full amount within twenty-four hours.[5]

Despite the services it rendered the Mother Lode and the Western frontier as a whole, in the fields of banking, express and transportation for businessman, miner and traveler alike, Wells Fargo was not always regarded with deep affection by the general public. In some quarters, Wells Fargo's charges were regarded as exorbitant taxes by a ruthless business monopoly. Also, the company's rewards to those who aided it during times of robbery were regarded as "pinch-penny." Consequently, the activities of bandits such as Black Bart were tolerated by too many otherwise honest Mother Lode citizens. Many looked upon these affairs simply as instances of one thief robbing another. Throughout California and the portions of Oregon and Nevada served by Wells Fargo, many were critical of what they considered niggling $100 rewards handed out by the company to citizens and even to its own employees who assisted in thwarting robberies or providing information that brought about arrests of bandits.

Commenting on Wells Fargo's rewards, the *Tuolumne Independent*, in an editorial later reprinted by the *Oakdale Wheat Grower*, stated, "It seems to us that by fair treatment, the company could gain sympathy of those people who live in the vicinity of the stage operations and make stage robbery a more dangerous pastime."

Jim Hume, also remarking on the lack of cooperation from the citizenry concerning stage robberies, quoted a resident of the town of Milton, who, when asked what he would do if he observed a stage being robbed, said, "Why I'd turn my back and walk away." No doubt it was the apathy of many people, rather than any outright dislike for Wells Fargo, that worked in favor of Black Bart. He was observed at various times, traveling through the mountains either immediately before or after a stage robbery. Seldom were these sightings hastily reported to authorities, if in fact they were reported at all.

One such sighting was finally reported decades too late to help Jim Hume. Toward the end of his life, William "Billy" Foster, who died in Auburn in 1928 at age seventy-one, often recalled that shortly before Christmas of 1881, he met a man he later realized was Black Bart. Foster said he was hydraulic mining on the Yuba River when a middle aged, mustached man who carried a satchel and thin blanket roll arrived at his cabin and spent two days with him, waiting out a storm. The man, who was friendly and talkative, according to Foster, claimed to be a Civil War veteran who had served under General Sherman during his march through Georgia. He left when the storm ended, saying he had to get to Plumas County, where a job as mine boss was waiting for him.

Foster said it was two weeks before he visited Marysville and heard of the robbery of the San Juan-Marysville stage a day or two after Christmas. Even then, he said, it was some time before he realized that his visitor had been the stage robber, Black Bart. "By then it was too late, so I didn't even bother telling the sheriff about the man who stayed with me," he said.[6]

It was nearly eight months after the Alturas-Redding stage robbery of October 27, 1879, that another robbery attributed to Black Bart occurred. On July 22, 1880, the Point Arena-Duncan Mills stage was robbed for the second time by a man then believed by some to have been the bandit Black Bart. But, there still remains question today, among history buffs of the stage robbery days, if that really was one of Bart's jobs.

Faced by a shotgun armed man in a mask, some four miles from Henry's Hotel, stage driver Martin McClennan told the gunman he could not throw down the express box because it was securely bolted to the floor of the stage. Then, following a hasty inspection, the bandit instructed McClennan to throw down the mail sacks–which he did–and then hurriedly drove on. If the stage robber was Black Bart, it was the first time he ever attempted a robbery without obtaining the express box. The empty mail sacks, letters scattered about them, were found next day in the bushes a short distance from where the robbery took place.

Casting doubt on the probability the robber was Black Bart was the testimony of the passengers, two men and a woman, who said they saw three accomplices. Jim Hume and other investigators discounted their claims and said they believed what the passengers had seen were sticks poking from behind rocks and bushes to simulate gun barrels–the old trick of Black Bart's. Also, adding to the doubt that Bart was involved in the holdup was the fact that a foot traveler, later that same day, reported he had been robbed by a masked man a few miles from Duncan Mills. Black Bart was never known during his eight-year career to rob an individual person. If indeed Bart was responsible, it would have meant he committed a string of twenty-nine robberies. It was not until years later, when Hume was in ill health and occupied with other problems, that Wells Fargo & Company officially attributed that robbery to Black Bart.

One of the reasons that Black Bart may have preferred the coastal area stages is that not being in the mining country, they carried cash instead of raw gold. Gold had to be exchanged for cash, and sometimes, astute gold buyers became suspicious of strangers who brought in sizable amounts of the precious yellow metal. Some of them reported these questionable transactions to law enforcement agencies, along with the descriptions of the sellers. It was just such a sale, during which a San Francisco gold buyer became suspicious, that led to the arrests of Billy Miner, Charlie Cooper and "Alkali Jim" Harrington for robbery of the San Andreas-Stockton stage in 1871. Also, some gold buyers could tell from its color and general characteristics where a particular type of gold came from. If a person brought them gold that was not from their local area, that also could lead to embarrassing questions. Black Bart was well aware of all those complications. Still another factor that may have made him lean toward areas outside the Mother Lode is that mining along the Sierra foothills in the 1880's was in decline except for the large mines. Too often, Wells Fargo boxes there were slim pickings, and those that did carry a rich cargo from the large mines were well-guarded.

Although he started late, 1880 was a busy year for Black Bart. On September 1, he stopped the Weaverville-Redding stage south of Last Chance Station, just inside the Shasta County line, took a Wells Fargo express box and the mail sacks, then rubbed salt into the wound by instructing stage driver Charley Creamer to give Jim Hume his best regards.

But Bart, at the same time, must have thought Wells Fargo was conspiring against him. For the second time in a row during the commission of a robbery he was forced to abandon his effort to open a treasure box carried on a stage.

After stopping the Weaverville-Redding stage Bart demanded and was given the wooden Wells Fargo express box and several mail pouches. However, he saw there was a second treasure box aboard and demanded that, too. The driver told him that was impossible, as it was bolted down, and anyway, it was made of iron and could not be broken open. Angered, Bart ordered the lone passenger, a woman, off the stage and went to work on the metal box with an axe. Finally, after pounding and prying on the box for several minutes, Bart was forced to give up and allow Creamer to proceed down the road with the second strong box unopened.[7] From the wooden express box that had been tossed down, Bart realized little more than one hundred dollars in cash. What he found in the mail sacks is unknown.

Following that robbery, Black Bart headed due south at a rapid pace, apparently traveling all night. A posse which left Redding trailed him a considerable distance before losing his track in the area of Eagle Creek. The Shasta County sheriff learned some days later that Bart had breakfasted at the remote Eagle Creek ranch of J. T. Adkinson. Bart told Adkinson and his family he was traveling cross-country to take a job as foreman in a Plumas County mine. He so impressed the Adkinsons with his good manners and easy humor that they sent him off with a package of sandwiches to tide him over until he reached the next settlement.

On September 16, little more than two weeks after his Weaverville-Redding stage robbery, Bart crossed the California-Oregon line to hit the Roseburg, Oregon-Yreka stage and make one of the largest hauls of his career. Once again, taking advantage of a moonlit night, Bart, wearing his usual flour sack mask, stopped the Yreka-bound stage shortly before midnight in the wild and unpopulated mountains only two miles north of the Oregon border.

Nort Eddings, who was handling the ribbons, drew his team up short when the masked man stepped into the dim lights of the stagecoach lanterns and ordered him to halt. Instructed to throw down the express box and mail bags, Eddings dropped the canvas sacks into the road but told the gunman the express box was chained inside the "boot" on the rear of the stage. This time, Bart was prepared for such eventualities. With what appeared in the darkness to be a large hammer or heavy axe, he broke open the express box without removing it from the boot and extracted in excess of one thousand dollars in raw gold and coin. According to the *Yreka Journal*, a large amount of cash also was taken from the mail.

Exactly one week later, on September 23, at almost the same spot on the Oregon side of the state line, the Roseburg stage was robbed again as it headed toward Yreka. That was a daylight robbery and again, nearly one thousand dollars was removed from the express box. The amount the bandit found in the mail was undetermined. There remains some confusion as to whether Nort Eddings was again the victim or if the stage was driven by George Chase. Bart departed the scene, leaving not a clue that would aid in tracking him down. Jim Hume was to find later that he had headed south and spent the night in a Paskenta, Tehama County, hotel where he registered as H. Barton. From there, he apparently headed for the comforts and safety of the bay area.

Although his recent undertakings had netted the elusive bandit fairly large amounts, stage robberies, like his earlier efforts at mining as a young man, were not making Black Bart rich. True, his periodic forays at the expense of Wells Fargo provided him with the wherewithal to lead, for varying intervals, the gentleman's life to which he aspired, but he never did make the big strike–the one big shipment of raw gold or minted coin that would have provided him the nest egg with which to retire. What his endeavors did net him was the undying enmity of Wells Fargo and the avowed determination of James Hume to bring him to justice. For Hume, it was a frustrating case. After each robbery Black Bart seemed to drop out of sight.

By the end of 1880 Hume and Jonathan Thacker, his chief aide, had developed a thick portfolio on Black Bart, the "Po8." However, they still lacked a good description of the man or any idea of who he was. Offers of reward brought no clues or information. Adding to Hume's problems of catching up with this robbery suspect was the fact that he ranged an area that extended over most of the northern portions of the state. Jim Hume was a professional. It rankled him that, unlike the many thieves and bandits he had put behind bars, this man who had dubbed himself Black Bart, simply left no tangible clues.

* * *

Hume, like the bandit he hunted, was born and raised on a New York State farm. As a young man, he had migrated with his family to La Grange County, Indiana. There he again was involved in farming until in 1850, at age twenty-three, he headed for California, lured by the cry of "Gold!"

Hume landed in Hangtown (Placerville) in the fall of 1850. His first years there were involved in mining and store keeping with varying degrees of success. The end of 1854 found him serving as an El Dorado County deputy sheriff-tax collector, and by 1862 he had become marshal and police chief of Placerville.

After a stint as El Dorado County under-sheriff, during which time, in 1864, he took part in hunting down Confederate states sympathizers who robbed a stage at Bullion Bend, near present-day Pollock Pines, Hume was elected sheriff of El Dorado County in 1860. Four years later, with stage robberies and embezzlements on the increase, Wells Fargo & Company hired him to head its force of special agents.

In addition to being recognized as one of California's best and most successful lawmen, Jim Hume was a person of aristocratic bearing. A handsome man, neat and well groomed, his appearance and quiet, efficient manner drew respect everywhere he went.

Years later, when the identity of Black Bart was known and he faced Jim Hume, those present, including Hume's friend and associate Jon Thacker, were struck with the resemblance of the two men.

Black Bart sported small, well trimmed chin whiskers. Hume had no beard, but both men wore flowing, well groomed mustaches and graying heads of hair. Hume was three inches taller than Bart, yet they shared similar facial characteristics.[8] Oddly enough, although one man was an outlaw and the other the epitome of law and order, both had the natural grace of gentlemen. Thacker, who was present when Hume and Black Bart met for the first time, noted that the two men could have passed as brothers.

Jim Hume had imagination as well as tenacity. He rightly surmised that Black Bart, while traveling to and from robbery sites, probably played upon the hospitality of mountain residents. Hume made polite inquiries of those folk and his assumption paid off in the fall of 1880, when Mrs. Sydney McCreary, wife of a Potter Valley rancher, recalled that in late June she had served lunch to a polite traveler whom she believed to have been an itinerant preacher.

Mrs. McCreary and her sixteen-year-old daughter, who had waited on the gentleman, were impressed with his obvious breeding, good manners, jokes and amusing conversation. They noted he did not smoke or appear to be a drinker, and after lunch he was profuse in his praise of the fine meal they had prepared for him.

With a housewife's eye, Mrs. McCreary noted that her guest's coat sleeve was crudely mended with white thread and his shoes were badly worn and split. His gold watch chain had been broken and was tied together with a leather thong. She described him as a man of medium height and build, with blue eyes, graying hair, bushy eyebrows and a somewhat bristly, almost white mustache which drooped slightly at the corners of his mouth. She said he had a slightly receding hairline and was missing at least two lower front teeth. Detective Hume said nothing, but he felt quite sure that this polite man was considerably more than a traveling minister who was down on his luck.[9]

A visit to Shasta County after the September 1, 1880 robbery of the Weaverville-Redding stage brought Jim Hume more information and a description of the suspected bandit which very closely matched that given by Mrs. McCreary. Eagle Creek rancher Adkinson, interviewed by Hume concerning the man who had breakfast with him, not only gave the same general picture of his guest that had been given by Mrs. McCreary, but he added that the friendly, gap-toothed man's hands showed little evidence of manual labor. James Hume was convinced that the traveler was the bandit who called himself Black Bart.

Also, in the fall of 1880, Hume learned that Redwood Valley farmer Elisha Shortridge–who lived about ten miles north of Ukiah, in the immediate area of several of Bart's robberies–had found cached in the woods near his home a blanket roll and valise containing a sawed-off, take-down model double barreled 12-gauge shotgun.

Hume also learned that at one point, a man of this same description had worked for a time at James Reed's sawmill on Shady Creek a few miles from present-day Grass Valley in Nevada County. Reed's sawmill was in an area that Black Bart would have traveled through to and from robberies in Yuba and Plumas Counties.

Black Bart ended 1880 with a November 20 holdup of the northbound Redding-Roseburg, Oregon stage and very nearly met his own end. Just at dusk Bart stepped into the road, pointed what stage driver Joe Mason identified as a rifle, and told him to throw down the express box and mail. Mason jettisoned the mail bags as ordered, but said the express box was too heavy for one man to lift from beneath the seat. Perhaps with visions of a heavy

Wells Fargo & Company express offices were spread throughout California, from primitive tent city mining camps to the prosperous foothill towns and metropolitan centers such as San Francisco, where its West Coast headquarters was located. This Wells Fargo office in the restored mining town of Columbia, in Tuolumne County, is especially well preserved.

shipment of gold coin or other valuables, Bart dropped his usual caution. He stepped up on the stage wheel, holding the gun in one hand, to offer Mason help with lifting the box. At that instant Mason grabbed a hatchet lying under his feet and swung, missing the bandit's masked head by a fraction of an inch. Frightened, Bart tumbled backward onto the road and fled, making no effort to use the gun. Mason drove on, and an hour later another stage driver traveling toward Redding found one of the slashed mail sacks in the road. The mail, according to local authorities, had contained little of value.

For Black Bart, 1881 was another busy year, if not a particularly lucrative one. Again, he allowed more than half the year to elapse before making his first move. Then, striking swiftly, he robbed three stages in little more than thirty days, confining his activities to the extreme northern portion of the state. If the word of witnesses can be believed, Bart also for the first time did not use the flour sack mask and instead had his face covered by a large handkerchief. He did, however, continue to wear the soiled tan duster that had become his trademark.

On August 31 he robbed the Roseburg-Yreka stage about nine miles north of Yreka. This was another nighttime robbery. Stage driver John Sullaway (some sources including the Pony Express spell it Lullaway) said he saw a small fire burning beside the road and thought he was coming upon a camp, when a man stepped out of the darkness, pointed a gun at him and told him to throw down the express box and mail sacks. Again, the express box was attached to the stage, but the bandit, who was wearing a duster, picked up an axe from the roadside and after telling Sullaway to stand at the heads of his lead horses, smashed open the box. Sullaway said that before he was allowed to climb back onto the stagecoach and drive on, he heard the bandit express disgust at how little he had found in the box. Postal authorities did not divulge how much might have been taken from the mail.

Where Black Bart may have spent the next month is unknown. It seems unlikely he would take off for San Francisco, which would require almost a week's travel, only to have to turn around and head back after a few days in order to be in the Redding area, where he robbed another stage on October 8.

The weather at that time of the year is generally good, and Bart could have camped out, moving slowly southward across the one hundred miles that separated the site of his August 31 robbery from the Buckeye-Hill Lake area where his October 8 robbery was to occur. But camping, particularly with minimal equipment, can become tiresome even for an experienced woodsman like Black Bart. Bart, in 1881, was nearly twenty years older than when he became accustomed to an outdoor existence during his Civil War days. Also, even under the best conditions, camping is dirty. Bart had learned to enjoy the amenities of city life, cleanliness, soft beds and prepared meals. It is possible, if he did not return to San Francisco between sessions with the caretakers of Wells Fargo treasure boxes, that he took refuge in a hotel or inn in some community located a considerable distance removed from his activities in the stage robbery business.

At any rate, the flour sack masked bandit stopped the stage headed from Redding to Yreka on the bright moonlit night of October 8, on Bass Hill, at about the same point he had robbed a stage two years earlier. Upon learning the express box was bolted to the floor of the boot, Bart instructed stage driver Horace Williams, like Sullaway, to climb down from the driver's box and stand by the heads of his lead horses. Brandishing his shotgun, he ordered the three passengers out of the stage and sent them walking down the road. After they had covered what he felt was a safe distance, Bart went to work on the express box with an axe and quickly smashed it open. Much to his chagrin, again the box held little of value. The Wells Fargo agent in Redding said the box had contained only sixty dollars, and Bart had to be content with what he found in the mail sacks.

Three days later, on the afternoon of October 11, stagecoach driver Lewis Brewster, headed south toward Redding from

Lakeview, Oregon and Alturas, stopped two miles north of Round Mountain to make a minor harness repair.

Suddenly he was startled by a man with a flour sack mask, wearing a soiled duster, who walked up behind him and demanded the express box and mail sacks. Brewster looked at the double barreled shotgun pointed at him and decided without further argument to follow orders. Brewster, who not only was a stage driver but also owned the Burney Valley way station, climbed onto the stage and angrily tossed down the box and sacks of mail. Then, still threatened by the shotgun, he drove on. However, after rounding the next couple of bends in the road, Brewster stopped the stage and with a rifle that had been concealed in the driver's box, he backtracked to the robbery scene, only to find that Black Bart had already fled. Because of his schedule and without anyone to watch his unattended team, Brewster was forced to break off the pursuit. Had he been able to continue, the Black Bart saga might have had a different ending. In 1876, as a member of a Trinity County sheriff's posse, Brewster had killed a bandit in a gun fight.[1]

Later, a posse that took up Bart's trail where Brewster left off scoured the country for more than sixty miles trying to pick up his track. Jim Hume suspected that Bart had headed for Oroville, then traveled by boat back to San Francisco. Wells Fargo again claimed the express box in the Round Mountain robbery contained only a small amount. What Bart may have found in the mail pouches is unknown.

For more than two months Black Bart laid low, then on December 15, 1881, possibly motivated by the fact his last four holdups had netted him small financial gain, he hit the Downieville-Camptonville-Marysville stage shortly after daylight in Yuba County, four miles north of Dobbins. Bart also appeared to have changed his gentlemanly attitude when calling for the Wells Fargo express box and mail, to one of forceful threat. During his early forays against stages, although he emphasized his demands with the muzzle of his double barreled shotgun, he had always asked the driver to "please throw down the box." But, on that cold morning of December 16, when he stopped the stage headed for Marysville, he told driver George Sharpe, "Throw down the box or I'll blow your damned head off!" Perhaps it was that change of approach—

Bart's adoption of the more belligerent attitude–that made James Hume wonder if another bandit had not also adopted use of the flour sack mask.

Sharpe said the stage robber, armed with a shotgun, jumped from behind a tree and ordered him to stop, but did most of his talking with his body at least partially shielded by the tree. His description fitted Black Bart closely, but there were discrepancies. Sharpe said the bandit wore a cloth mask with a tear in it rather than a flour sack with eye holes. Through the tear he said he could determine the gunman had blue eyes, light or graying hair, and wore a small gray hat. Another part of the description that varied was that the bandit was using a muzzle loading shotgun. Sharpe was emphatic in describing the gun, stating he could see its exposed percussion caps–the definite mark of a muzzle loader. In all his past holdups, Bart always had employed a modern, double barreled breech loader.

Still another point that made identity of the stage robber questionable was that during the holdup he used considerable profanity while demanding that the express box and mail pouches be thrown down. That in itself was totally unlike Black Bart, who was noted for his polite approach while conducting a robbery. At any rate, according to Wells Fargo, he got not a dime from the express box.

After the robbery, as Sharpe followed the bandit's instructions to drive on, a small boy riding beside him pulled a modest package from beneath his coat and said, "Well, at least they didn't get this."

"What is it?" asked the still somewhat startled driver.

"That's my lunch," replied the youngster.

Later, commenting on the robbery and Wells Fargo's minimal loss, Jim Hume said, "That stage robber would have been better off if he'd left the Wells Fargo box and taken the kid's lunch."

The following day the *Marysville Appeal* printed one of the longer and more descriptive Black Bart stories in its account of the robbery of the Downieville-Marysville stage. The story also shows that Bart was beginning to take at least some precaution against stopping a bullet and that he definitely had, unless the driver was exaggerating, dropped his earlier courtesy toward stage drivers. The following story appeared December 17 in the Marysville paper:

The Camptonville Stage Robbed

A Masked Highwayman Gets Away With The Express Box and the U.S. Mails.

The down stage from Camptonville was stopped by a robber about four miles above Dobbin's Ranch yesterday morning, and the mails and express box taken. George Sharpe, the driver of the stage, gave this account of the affair to an APPEAL reporter last evening:

"I was driving slowly up a bit of rising ground when suddenly a man jumped out from behind a tree by the side of the road and yelled: 'Hold on there you – – –. I pulled up the horses pretty quick and set the brake. Then I sat still and looked at the man. I had never been stopped on the road before, and was surprised like. The man was about my size, [pretty stoutly built and about 5 feed 10 inches high.] His face was covered with white cotton cloth, but one corner of the cloth was torn so that I could see that his eyes were blue. He had on a long linen duster and a pair of blue overalls. On his head was a little whitish felt hat, with some light colored hair sticking out through the crown. That's about all I remember of his looks. He spoke in a clear, ringing voice, without any brogue or foreign accent. There was a double-barreled muzzle-loading shotgun in his hands. I could see the caps on the nipples. I saw all these things in a good deal less time than it takes to tell about them. As soon as I stopped the horses the robber got back behind the tree, so as to keep out of range of any guns that the passengers might have. He kept his shotgun bearing down on me from the word 'Hold.' 'Throw out that box.' was his next order. I supposed he meant the Wells-Fargo box, but I didn't stop to make particular inquiries, and I threw it out on the side of the road towards him. 'Now throw out the other box, and be quick, – – you.' he said. 'This line packs only one Wells-Fargo box.' 'Well, then, throw out them, – – you,' he said. 'That's all there is,' I said, thinking it a matter of principle to lie, under the circumstances. Then he gave his gun a flourish, squinted along the top of the barrels at me, and yelled out, 'None of your – funny business. Sling out that mail quick, or I'll blow the top of your – head off, you – – –, you.' It seemed the proper thing to throw out the rest of the mail and, and I did so. 'Now drive on, you – – –, he said. I drove on. He kept me covered with the shotgun until the corner of the coach shut me out of range, and then he brought the gun to bear on the passengers inside. There were five of them, all Chinamen. I never heard such a pow-wow as those Chinamen made when they saw the gun pointed at them. There was a white boy on the box seat with me. He was badly scared. After I had driven on a piece, he said to me, 'I'm glad that robber didn't get my parcel,' showing a little package wrapped up in a newspaper. 'What have you in that,' I asked him. 'I've got my lunch in it,' he said. And that was all the poor little cuss did have in it."

A telegram was received from Camptonville at Wells, Fargo & Co.'s agency here last evening, stating that here was no money in the express box taken from the stage. It is not known whether or not there was any money in the mail bags. Probably there was. Deputy Sheriff Aldrich starts out this morning for the scene of the robbery.

On December 27, 1881, after the end of the storm during which Yuba River gold miner Billy Foster gave a man answering Black Bart's description shelter for a couple of days, the San Juan-Smartsville stage was robbed four miles north of Smartsville. The bandit's description closely fit that of Black Bart, but his take was so trivial that even the local newspapers gave it little space. The Wells Fargo agent in San Juan claimed the express box was virtually empty and the loss from the mail sack was said to be small. The robbery was of such little consequence the papers did not even identify the stage driver.

Bart's ability to choose stages without armed guards continued. Perhaps his good judgment was due solely to luck, or perhaps he spied on the stages from ambush and chose not to confront those which carried a messenger. Some gangs, during the 1870's and '80's, reportedly operated with lookouts located at a point where they could observe an oncoming stage–sometimes with the aid of a spy glass–and signal their companions as to whether it carried a guard. One such lookout on the North Fork of the American River, overlooking the present Lake Clementine, still is known locally as "Robber's Roost."[2] From that huge limestone outcropping an outlaw could watch the gold-laden stages traveling the old North Fork Grade from Foresthill, Todds Valley and Michigan Bluff and signal his gang members as they waited in hiding.

Still other sophisticated gangs supposedly had "plants" who were employed in positions that would allow them to know when a valuable shipment of gold was being put aboard a stage. Bart, working alone, had none of those refinements available to him. Luck or skill, Bart usually did not challenge guarded stages, and that probably is why he never hit a really big shipment. It also is probably why, through twenty-eight or twenty-nine robberies, he managed to stay alive. Certainly, after July 13, 1882, he had good reason to leave the guarded stages assiduously alone.

With winter bearing down, Black Bart returned to San Francisco after his near fruitless December 27 robbery of the San Juan-Smartsville stage. However, because neither the San Juan stage venture or the several preceding holdups had produced much in the way of profits for him, late January found Bart back in the mountains, returning to his trade. He was doing so even though winter travel was difficult and he was fully aware that a man's tracks are easier to follow in wet soil. The truth was, he needed the money.

This time Bart changed locations and returned to Mendocino County. There, on January 26, 1882, almost a month to the day after his Smartsville holdup, he stopped the Ukiah-Cloverdale stage and made off with the valuables from two Wells Fargo express boxes and several sacks of mail. Exactly why there were two express boxes on the stage never was explained by Wells Fargo.

The robbery occurred during the late afternoon about six miles north of Cloverdale when Bart, reported by stage driver Harry Forse to have been armed with a rifle, hailed him down and demanded the express boxes and mail. Forse was traveling alone without a guard or passengers. He dropped the boxes and mail bags, then drove rapidly to a toll station less than a mile down the road. Toll station operator Joseph A. Lance and several others grabbed guns and returned to the point of the robbery, only to find broken express boxes, slashed mail sacks, and the bandit gone. They tracked the stage robber for a distance, but with darkness falling, were forced to give up the chase. Posses also were sent out from Ukiah and from Hopland, but the fleeing bandit was too far ahead of them.

Local newspapers, quoting Wells Fargo agents, said approximately three hundred dollars was taken from the express boxes. It appears that considerably more may have been found in the mail, for it was early summer before Black Bart decided to make another withdrawal from Wells Fargo.

Apparently well bank-rolled, he abandoned the mountains. Once again, under the alias of Charles Bolton, mining man, he headed south to take up the good life in San Francisco. For the next six months, until June 14, he would lead the life of an affluent gentleman.

Bolton enjoyed the theater and the city's better restaurants. He was not unknown at such places as the Palace Hotel and the Opera House. Among his favorite haunts was William Pike's New York Restaurant and Bakery on Kearney Street, not far from San Francisco's police headquarters. The bakery was a favorite hangout of detectives, many of whom, like Detective David Scannell, had become good friends with Bolton. When his overcoat was stolen one night from the hotel where he had stayed for a time, detectives Bill Jones and Daniel Coffey recovered it for him. He tipped them and thanked them graciously.[3]

Charles Bolton had no fear of his true identity's being found out, for he had no criminal record and associated only with people of high respectability. No one had ever seen his face during the commission of a robbery and to his knowledge, no one in law enforcement had a description of his physical features.

As Charles Bolton, prosperous mine owner and mining engineer, he fully enjoyed the life of a boulevardier. He was an avid reader and frequented a book shop owned by a man named Alec Robertson where he was a favored customer. In the city he always appeared in public well dressed. With bowler hat, stylish wide cravat and diamond stickpin, well tailored tweed suit, velvet collared topcoat and cane, he was the epitome of the successful business executive. His flowing white mustache, heavy gold watch chain and diamond ring added to this air of wealth and dignity. Although he had resided in other of the city's hostelries, he considered the Webb House, at 37 Second Street, his permanent address.

Perhaps it was his previous military service that gave him his erect and alert bearing and made the man who called himself Bolton seem taller than his true five feet nine inches. Physically, he kept himself in top shape, and although he apparently had few if any intimate female friends, women found him handsome. A clever conversationalist with a wide range of interests, he appeared well educated and conversed fluently on a variety of subjects. Bolton also possessed a sharp sense of humor and, according to those who knew him, made friends easily.

* * *

Late in 1849, at age twenty, this future bandit,[4] whose real name was Charles Boles, left for California with his brother, David. After wintering in Missouri, probably in Independence or Saint Joseph, they arrived in the gold fields in the early fall of 1850. Their first mining endeavors were on the North Fork of the American River. What their fortune was there is not recorded, but they moved on to mine in Butte, El Dorado and Tuolumne counties, then turned north to Shasta and Trinity, where they mined with some success before returning to New York.

The two brothers' stay in the East appears brief, for the summer of 1852 found them back in California. However, on July 9, 1852, before they were able to leave San Francisco to go mining, David Boles became ill and died. He was interred in San Francisco's Yerba Buena Cemetery.

Once again, Charles Boles tried mining, but soon gave it up and headed east. That time he did not return to New York, and 1854 found him in Decatur, Illinois. There he settled down and soon married. By 1861, when the Civil War erupted, Boles and his wife, Mary, had two daughters.

On September 6, 1862, Boles enlisted[5] in the Union Army and was assigned to Company B, 116th Illinois Volunteer Infantry. Boles saw his first combat at Chickasaw Bayou, on the Yazoo River in Mississippi. Soon after, in early January, 1863, Company B took heavy casualties in the Battle of Arkansas Post. At the end of that fight, Company B could muster only twenty-five men, Boles among them, who were fit for duty.

Agents of W., F. & Co. will not post this circular, but place them in the hands of your local and county officers, and reliable citizens in your region. Officers and citizens receiving them are respectfully requested to preserve them for future reference.

Agents WILL PRESERVE a copy on file in their office.

$800.00 Reward!

ARREST STAGE ROBBER!

1.

On the 3d of August, 1877, the stage from Fort Ross to Russian River was stopped by one man, who took from the Express box about $300, coin, and a check for $305.52, on Grangers' Bank of San Francisco, in favor of Fisk Bros. The Mail was also robbed. On one of the Way Bills left with the box the Robber wrote as follows:—

"I've labored long and hard for bread—
For honor and for riches—
But on my corns too long you've trod,
You fine haired sons of bitches.
BLACK BART, the P o 8.

Driver, give my respects to our friend, the other driver; but I really had a notion to hang my old disguise hat on his weather eye." (fac simile.)

It is believed that he went to the Town of Guerneville about daylight next morning.

2.

About one year after above robbery, July 25th, 1878, the Stage from Quincy to Oroville was stopped by one man, and W., F. & Co's box robbed of $379, coin, one Diamond Ring, (said to be worth $200) one Silver Watch, valued at $25. The Mail was also robbed. In the box, when found next day, was the following. (fac simile):—

Confidential circular mailed by Wells Fargo detective James Hume to Wells Fargo agents throughout Northern California following the August 3, 1877, Duncan Mills stage robbery. This circular, like others sent out later, produced no clues.

43

In May, 1864, Sgt. Boles received a severe abdominal wound during fighting at Dallas, Georgia. Following his recovery, he returned to the ranks and saw combat at Vicksburg, Chattanooga, Kenesaw Mountain and Atlanta. He actually was promoted to the rank of second lieutenant, but the war ended before he received his commission. He was discharged near Washington, D.C., shortly after the end of the war.

A civilian again, Charles Boles returned to his wife and children to take up farming near New Oregon, Iowa. It did not take him long to become disillusioned with what was proving to be a hand-to-mouth farming life. Some time in 1867, as Boles approached the age of 40, he left Mary and his daughters and headed for Montana or Idaho to once again take up gold mining.

Some months after arriving in Montana, Boles wrote his wife that he was coming home, then changed his mind.

He wrote periodically and from time to time sent her small sums of money. Supposedly Mary Boles was earning a meager living by taking in sewing, but Boles later claimed that his father, who was well off, took care of Mary's financial needs during that period. James Hume would, in his later years, contend that long before Boles, as Black Bart, began his stage robbery career, he had dastardly abandoned his wife and children.

Two years later, in 1869, Boles wrote to his wife and told her he had just purchased a promising Idaho mining claim. Apparently, the Boles gold mine did not prosper. He wrote to his wife from Silver Bow, Montana, in August, 1871, then moved on to Salt Lake City. From Utah, he drifted back to California.

There are stories that Boles taught school during the early 1870's in Sierra and Contra Costa counties, but these reports remain unconfirmed.

* * *

Some time in early June, 1882, Charles Boles, known to his West Coast friends as Charles E. Bolton and to Jim Hume as Black Bart, left San Francisco for the mountains, carrying a thin bedroll and a battered leather valise.

On June 14, three miles from Little Lake, a man wearing a flour sack mask stepped into the road in front of the Little Lake-Ukiah stage. He leveled a double barreled shotgun at driver Thomas B. Forse, brother of Harry Forse, whom a similarly masked bandit had robbed just six months before.

As he already had in the past, during that holdup Black Bart encountered the Wells Fargo innovation which, although it had not put a stop to stage robbery, made it considerably more difficult: the iron express box.

During its early years in California, the company transported the treasure entrusted to it in sturdily built, strap-iron reinforced wooden boxes built by San Francisco cabinet maker Joseph William Ayer.[6] Those express boxes, twenty inches long, twelve inches wide and ten inches high, weighed twenty-four pounds and rode on the floor of the front "boot," beneath the feet of the driver. They were stout enough that without a key to provide access, they had to be smashed open with an axe or hammer. These were the boxes that the highwaymen who preyed on Wells Fargo referred to when they issued that often-heard peremptory order: "Throw down the box!"

Soon however, as stage robberies increased, the express company began switching to iron boxes that required considerably more effort on the part of the bandits to reach their contents. On stage routes where transportation of large amounts of coin or gold bullion was common, the company had iron stage safes built that rode under the rear seat of the coach or were bolted to the floor of its rear boot.

In one instance on the Sonora-Milton stage run in Calaveras County, bandits, after stopping one of Joe Dechamp's stages, attempted to open the iron safe bolted into the rear boot by blasting it with a charge of black powder. The resulting explosion destroyed the rear end of the stage but failed to open the safe.

To make the situation even less attractive for stage robbers, the company also began bolting down even the small express boxes.

At the range of thirty feet, the muzzle of a double barreled 12-gauge shotgun has impelling powers of persuasion. Without argument, Thomas Forse halted the stage, but when instructed to throw down the express box, he was unable to comply.

"I can't," he informed the gunman. "The box is bolted down."

Although he was not pleased, Black Bart again was fully prepared to deal with that situation. He ordered Forse down from the stage, then after making sure he was unarmed, instructed him to unhitch the team of horses, lead them down the road and not to return for one hour. As driver and horses rounded the next bend, Bart climbed onto the stage and attacked the metal express box with a heavy hammer and chisel-bitted steel bar.

Exactly where Black Bart spent the next thirty days is not known, but early July found him in Plumas County, involved in his twenty-fourth stage robbery. As between robberies in the Fall of the previous year, it is unlikely he would have returned to San Francisco for such a relatively short period of time and it is doubtful he would have chanced moving into some small mountain or foothill community where, as a stranger, he would have stood out.

On rare occasions he accepted shelter for a night or two at remote homesteads, but since the weather would be mild in the summer, he probably camped in some isolated area, possibly not far from where he planned his next holdup. Perhaps he had a camping outfit and food cached somewhere in the mountains.

The privation experienced in the field during his army years that may have prepared Bart for the rigors of existing in the mountains with little more than nothing while on his stage robbery campaigns. Apparently he lived on the little he carried with him, mostly dry food that could be eaten without cooking. There are few if any authenticated reports of his visiting stores or trading posts to replenish supplies during his early robbery years. In rare instances Bart stopped at isolated ranches or cabins, where he was invited to a meal, and on occasion stayed overnight as he did at Billy Foster's cabin during a storm.

Bart traveled the Sierra and the Coast Range mountains winter and summer, his only shelter one or two blankets. Seldom, if he is to be believed, did he build a fire. Campfires in the woods, even during the 1870's and '80's, tended to attract unwanted attention.

At times, either before or immediately after a robbery, Bart hiked cross-country forty or fifty miles through mountainous terrain in a single day. Only those who have traveled trailless back country can appreciate what a feat of endurance that really is. If Black Bart can be given credit for nothing else, he at least proved himself a superb woodsman and survivor.

On the morning of July 13, 1882, nine miles from Strawberry, the familiar flour sacked masked figure stepped into the path of the LaPorte-Oroville stage which was carrying $23,000 in gold. Ignoring the armed guard riding beside driver George Helm, the bandit pointed a shotgun squarely at Helm and politely instructed him to throw down the box.[7]

The flour sack hooded man standing there in the road was just too enticing a target for messenger George Hacket to resist. As the bandit brandished his shotgun in front of the lead horses and waited for Helm to throw down the heavy box, Hacket raised his rifle and fired. At best, it was a snap shot, for Hacket had to raise his rifle and fire in one almost instantaneous movement before the bandit could pull the trigger of his shotgun. Adding to Hacket's problem, the stage robber's body was shielded by the horses, and Hacket had to hold his sights high on the man's flour sack covered head in order to avoid hitting the animals.

At the report of the rifle the bandit, without returning fire, whirled and disappeared into the trees that screened the road's edge. Hacket jumped from the stage and gave chase. He was unable to rundown the robber, but a short distance from the road he found the flour sack mask and a bloodstained, bullet-punctured hat. For the remainder of his life, C. E. Boles, alias Charles Bolton, alias Black Bart, bore a narrow scar along the top of his right temple. Since this man, known as Black Bart, was no stranger to gunfire, having spent four years in combat in America's bloodiest war, it is quite probable that he did not return Hacket's fire because, as he later contended, he never carried a loaded shotgun in any of his twenty-eight robberies.

For little more than two months after his narrow escape in the LaPorte-Oroville stage robbery attempt, Black Bart laid low. How he explained to friends his newly acquired scalp wound is not known. Quite possibly he attributed it to some mining accident. Certainly, few of his San Francisco associates would ever connect this well mannered man of apparent means with such a thing as crime or a bullet wound.

Not long deterred by his close brush with death, on September 17, Bart stopped the Yreka-Redding stage fourteen miles out of Redding, and for the second time in two years encountered stage driver Horace Williams. The reunion did not exactly fill

47

Williams with delight, but he was traveling without a messenger, and there was nothing he could do but turn over the express box and mail sack to the shotgun toting bandit.

Black Bart's last robbery of 1882 occurred November 23, on the Lakeport-Cloverdale run. He ordered driver Dick Crawford and several passengers off the stage, then forced them to unhook the horses and lead them up the road. Waiting until they were out of sight, he pried open the metal express box and rifled the mail.

It is not clear how much Bart realized from either the September or the November robberies, but probably it was not a great deal. The glory days were over in the mining areas. In areas such as Lakeport and Cloverdale, which were outside the gold country, the transportation of coin and currency had diminished as postal money orders came into more common use. The use of money orders had made the U.S. Mail much less lucrative for road agents.

Not until Black Bart's stage robbery career had drawn to a close near the end of 1883 did anyone, including James Hume and the other lawmen who had hunted him, realize he had committed at least twenty-eight separate stage holdups. Only when Hume and Calaveras County Sheriff Ben Thorn questioned Bart at length and assured him of immunity from prosecution did they learn the full extent of his depredations against Wells Fargo. Then, seated in the relative comfort of the Calaveras County Sheriff's Office, assured his revelation of additional robberies would not be used against him, Bart became cautiously willing to talk. In fact, as he outlined the details of one robbery after another, his voice took on something of an air of pride in how smoothly they had been pulled off.[1]

"We knew he was telling the truth because he related the details of each robbery that were never known to the public," said Hume. "His memory was good and he told us the fine points of each holdup. Yet, there were many things that this man who had called himself Black Bart did not divulge. For instance, where and with whom he stayed after he received the scalp wound from George Hammett's rifle bullet during the attempted robbery of the LaPorte-Marysville stage."

Freight wagons such as this with its two trailers drawn by a 16-horse jerk line team near the outskirts of Angels Camp, brought supplies to the Mother Lode and at times, provided a slow, but safe method of travel for men who were on the dodge and wanted to escape to the area without being observed or leaving tracks.

Although Bart never was known to have committed a stage robbery in gold-rich Placer or El Dorado counties, he was seen there on at least one occasion. One reason for his not attempting any robberies there may have been that stages in those counties, when carrying any real amount of treasure, were usually accompanied by one or more armed messengers.

The late John DeMaria, of Foresthill, Placer County, often recalled that during the early 1880's, quite possibly just before Bart's robbery of the Jackson-Ione stage in 1883, he was believed to have been seen near Todd's Valley, traveling south toward El Dorado and Amador counties. DeMaria said his grandmother, Mrs. Ferrier, fed a small, neatly dressed gentleman who stopped at her ranch to ask directions to the Ford's Bar Trail that led to the American River and on into El Dorado County, near Georgetown. She said the middle-aged, mustached man looked hungry, and knowing that he would have to travel a long distance

before reaching the next settlement, she offered him a sandwich which he politely accepted.

Bart also confided to Sheriff Thorn and Hume that on occasion, while traveling the mining country, particularly during winter storms, he sometimes caught a ride on one of the huge freight wagons that hauled supplies to the towns and mining camps in the gold country. The freight wagon with its canvas top provided shelter from rain and snow, and its high sides also provided concealment from prying eyes of other travelers or law enforcement men.[2]

The teamsters, whose tandem-hitched freight wagons were pulled by teams of eighteen or twenty big mules or draft horses, probably paid little attention to an inoffensive appearing, middle-aged man who asked politely if he could ride a few miles to rest his weary feet. Even if they suspected that the man who climbed into one of the wagons might have been more than just a sore-footed traveler, many of them would not have gone out of their way to tell the local sheriff or Wells Fargo agent of their suspicions.

There was no great amount of love lost between the drivers of those jerkline freight teams and the flamboyant drivers of the

Concord stagecoaches or Henderson mud wagons that carried Wells Fargo express boxes and went churning by "hell-fer-leather" in a cloud of dust. It was always the freight teamster, laboring up some steep, winding grade, who had to pull over to allow the speeding stagecoach to pass. If a stagecoach and freight wagon, both in need of repair, pulled up to the blacksmith shop at some remote way station, it was always the stage that received its repairs first.

For the stage driver, the forty-mile trip from Marysville to LaPorte, Sonora to Milton, or Auburn to Georgetown or Foresthill, was an easy, one-day run. For the driver of a jerkline team pulling two freight wagons loaded with up to five tons of merchandise ranging from flour to flat-irons to cast iron stoves, ten to fourteen miles was a good day's travel. Those trips, hot and dusty in summer, muddy and freezing cold in winter for the freighters and their animals, made way stations along the route where they could put up for the night imperative for man and beast. It was for the freight traffic, not the stage lines, that way stations with colorful names like Mountain Gate, Butcher Ranch, Grizzly Bear House, Hawk Eye Station and Pool Station sprang up along the roads leading to the mining country.

Although the job of stage driver was a coveted one, surrounded with more than a degree of excitement and glamour, that of the freight teamster contained neither romance nor excitement. His job meant simply hard work and long hours, while demanding all, or even more, of the skills and expertise of the stage driver.

Each twenty-four hours was the same. They drove all day, stopping at one station if they could, for a noon meal and to rest and water their horses. They arrived at another station that night, often as darkness fell, but before they could eat or rest, their animals had to be cared for. There were harness galls to inspect and treat, cracked hooves to grease, or a loosened shoe to be reset. If the horses were too warm, each animal had to be rubbed down. Only then did the teamster take time out for, possibly, a drink or two and to eat supper and maybe, before heading to bed, to chew the fat with fellow teamsters or travelers.

It was a ritual among freight drivers that each night before rolling into bed they would make a final inspection of their horses or mules, checking each animal individually.[3] A sick horse often meant staying up all night, or at best, bedding down on a nearby bale of hay and sleeping with one eye open to make sure the animal was going to be all right.

A driver arose long before daybreak and went to the stable where his horses were quartered to feed, water, curry and harness them. Then, with that chore completed, the driver went back to the way station or hotel, grabbed whatever might be available to eat, and, often still in darkness, was on his way.

Men like Jim Sheridan, who freighted out of Auburn, Ben Green, who as a young man drove to the mines around Foresthill, and Andy Johnson, who drove freight teams in Amador and Calaveras counties, were respected by the men who hired them and by the community at large. In fact, these men who kept the supplies rolling into the foothills were often more respected by the general populace than the more colorful stage drivers who took off in a cloud of dust, seldom if ever drove the same team two days in a row, and left the care of their horses to stable hostlers.

If the freighters looked a bit disdainfully at the stage drivers and their little four- and six-horse rigs, and maybe didn't seem too sympathetic when they heard of some bandit, such as Black Bart, relieving a stage driver of his Wells Fargo box, it was not too difficult to see why.

Wherever there was freight travel or stage lines there were way stations of various sizes providing varying levels of material comforts. All offered food, sometimes of questionable palatability, and a place to sleep, although too often with more than a fair share of fleas and other small critters. As testimony to this, the town of Ione, in Amador County, during its early years was known as "Bedbug."

Early in his career Black Bart occasionally stayed at way stations, but in later years he mostly left them alone. Bart's personal fastidiousness probably was a factor in his avoidance of the stopping places. He no doubt felt the woods were considerably cleaner, and, more important of course, woodland hideouts contained no prying eyes or curious proprietors. Bart knew too well that strangers who stopped at way stations were invariably subjected to close scrutiny by both the owners and any hangers-on.

Jim Hume was well aware of that, too, and he was puzzled and frustrated by the lack of any real clues produced by reward offers that had climbed to the heady sum of eight hundred dollars. Surely, he figured, more information should be drifting into his office from distant way stations and crossroads settlements where some proprietor had observed a suspicious stranger who had stopped by or stayed overnight. Nor was Hume convinced all of the robberies being attributed to Black Bart were being conducted by one man. He suspected that some stage drivers, Wells Fargo agents and some local lawmen had been overcome by "Black Bart Fever." A realist, Hume didn't believe one man could cover so great an area in so short a time or pull so many robberies without getting caught or shot. Near the close of Bart's career, Hume only thought him responsible for about twenty robberies.

Another factor that bothered Hume was the amount of time he and his agents were spending on the Black Bart case. Actually, the amount of money Wells Fargo had lost due to Bart's robberies was not nearly as great as its losses in some single train robberies. What Bart was really stealing, Hume realized, was the time he and his men should have been devoting to the growing number of train robberies in the West.

For Hume, it was a frustrating situation. To ignore the Black Bart robberies was an impossibility. Furthermore, each one that was committed and not followed by an arrest invited others to take up the highwayman's trade. He divided his time between hurried trips to northern California whenever a stage holdup occurred, and longer trips to Arizona, Nevada and Oregon to investigate thefts and robberies there.[4] One of the crimes the Wells Fargo Company would not tolerate and would go to almost any lengths to bring a suspect to justice, was internal theft by its agents or office employees. But these cases required time and travel. They, along with train robberies which were becoming increasingly serious, kept Hume and his men constantly on the jump.

Each stage robbery was duly noted by the press with stories, of varied length and detail, depending on the publication and, of course, the importance of the robbery itself. Wells Fargo spokesmen, quite willing to make it known if a robbed express box had contained no funds, were reticent to mention the amount of the loss if the box contained treasure.

For instance, the *Oroville Mercury* gave Black Bart's July 25 Quincy-Oroville and his July 30, 1878 LaPorte-Oroville stage robberies only minimum space in a combined story printed August 2. The paper noted the masked bandit's take in the first robbery amounted only to some five hundred dollars in checks. The story did not divulge the amount lost by Wells Fargo in the LaPorte-Oroville holdup. However, it related that after the shotgun-wielding bandit forced stage driver Charlie Sherman to throw down the box, Mrs. Sam Wheeler, wife of LaPorte's Wells Fargo agent, who was riding beside Sherman, shouted to the stage robber, "Take it, you scoundrel, if it will do you any good!" The story stated that the express box had contained only a relatively small amount of cash, "but it means more work for the sagacious Mr. Hume."

The main thing about the robberies that irked northern California lawmen and Wells Fargo Detective Chief Jim Hume in particular, was their inability to find out who Black Bart really was. Every sheriff, every policeman, every prison official has his stable of informers—and that was just as true in 1880 as it is today. Yet not a word drifted in from the crime world to identify the "Po8" that was preying on the stages.

The reason, Sheriff Thorn, Jim Hume and others would learn much later, was that no one knew anything to tell. Black Bart had no criminal record, he did not consort with criminals or people of bad character. He had no accomplices and he confided in no one.

During an interview with a San Francisco newsman, Jim Hume discussed crimes against Wells Fargo, stage robbery in particular. "In the majority of stage robberies we can pretty soon pick up a clue to the party or parties who have done the job," said Hume. "Frequently, in fact, we can name them at once and run them down with a reasonable time." That, of course, was not true of the bandit that James Hume knew as Black Bart.

The trouble was, simply, Hume, his special agents and the sheriffs were looking in the wrong place. They were seeking the kind of a robber with whom they were familiar—some marginally educated indigent turned criminal who already had spent time in jail and had a criminal record. A criminal who associated with other criminals and who, when he made a lucky strike, be it in mining or in the opening of a Wells Fargo express box, went on a spree and threw money to the birds.

Had James Hume, en route to or from his office on a busy San Francisco street, met the man he was looking for face to face, it is likely the detective would have simply nodded a greeting to the well dressed, middle-aged gentleman and gone on his way.

During later conversations with Hume and Thorn, Bart revealed some of the areas where he had hidden out both before and after his robberies. He did not, however, divulge the names of people with whom he had stayed, although Hume eventually was able to learn the identity of some of them. None of those who had befriended Bart and given him food and shelter had even a vague idea of who he really was or the real reason for his travels. He most often passed himself off as a miner going to or from his claim. To be convincing, he said, he sometimes carried a few dollars worth of raw gold. "This gave me real authenticity," he said, "but I never carried enough gold to make them greedy."

Two things that made Bart welcome at remote ranches and cabins were his ability as a conversationalist and that he was the bearer of news from the outside world. Another was that he could be a good worker. At one point he worked for a time on a Nevada County ranch where the owner operated a small sawmill. When Bart decided to move on, the rancher-lumber mill owner begged him to stay.

Western historian Richard Dillon, in his biography of James Hume, quotes veteran driver Sam Smith, when his Sonora-Milton stage was robbed during the 1880's, as stating that his express box was empty and "Wells Fargo boxes are young poor houses on this road right now. You couldn't squeeze a picayune out of one of them to save your sweet neck from the gallows."

From November 1882 until April 1883 Black Bart refrained from any further robberies while presumably enjoying life in San Francisco. And, although Jim Hume now possessed a good description of him, he had not been able to turn up another single clue as to the identity or whereabouts of his prime robbery suspect. Then, on April 12, 1883, five miles from Cloverdale, on the Lakeport-Cloverdale Road, Black Bart robbed a stage driven by Bill Connibeck. The stage had no shotgun messenger and Bart escaped unscathed with the meager contents of both the express box and mail sacks. Cloverdale Wells Fargo agent Charles Aull, in a message to Hume in San Francisco, said, "The robber without a doubt is Black Bart. The mail sacks are cut the same as in all the robberies he has committed." And, what stage driver Sam Smith had said concerning the paucity of valuables carried in Wells Fargo express boxes on the Sonora-Milton run also proved true at Cloverdale. Bart's take from both the express box and the mail bags amounted to something less than fifty dollars.

June 23 found Black Bart back in the Mother Lode, where in Amador County, four miles west of Jackson, he robbed the Jackson-Ione stage driven by Clint Radcliffe. This time Bart's take probably was considerable, for several mines in the Jackson-Sutter Creek area still were producing well and quite regularly shipped fairly large amounts of gold. In addition, Jackson was a busy foothill town and the mail bags which Black Bart appropriated along with the Wells Fargo box probably contained considerable cash. Bart escaped into the rolling oak and chemise brush-covered hills, leaving not a trace. Actually, he was only about forty miles from Sacramento and, traveling back roads and trails, he could have made his way there fairly easily.

Radcliffe, a career driver, would gain prominence when, ten years later, on June 15, 1893, at almost exactly the same spot on the stage run, an unidentified rifleman stepped from behind a tree and killed famed shotgun messenger Mike Tovey, riding beside him. Radcliffe, braving the gunfire, grasped the dying Tovey and held him to prevent his falling from the stage while he drove the coach out of danger. Although a man was arrested and ultimately sent to prison for Tovey's slaying, Wells Fargo officials, including James Hume, did not believe he was the guilty man. The case remained in Wells Fargo's records as an unsolved murder.

Although it might appear that by the 1880's with more stages on the road than in earlier years, the pickings for holdup men would have been easier, just the opposite was true. Virtually all of the stage lines in the gold country were privately owned, and Wells Fargo contracted with only a few of them to transport its express boxes. Thus, an outlaw who at gunpoint waved down a fast traveling mud wagon might find himself facing only frightened passengers which included women and children, and his entire take if he robbed them might amount to only a few dollars.

The owners of the stage lines that carried Wells Fargo treasure also were becoming more prudent concerning protection of the boxes. Now, on most stages, the express box no longer rode beneath the driver's feet, but was bolted to the floor inside the coach. And, not always did the shotgun messenger ride up on the seat beside the driver where, not only was he vulnerable to gunfire, but his presence served notice that the stage was under guard. Instead, if the coach was not crowded, the guard often rode inside where, indistinguishable from the passengers, he was able to draw an undisturbed bead on an unsuspecting bandit.

One such incident occurred during the 1890's when Bob Murphy, nineteen, and a twenty-year-old man named Westfall attempted to rob a stage on the outskirts of Angels Camp which had two guards riding in it. The shotgun of one of the guards misfired, but guard Fred Jackson put a .44 caliber bullet through Murphy's chest. Westfall fled at the firing of the first shot but was arrested the next day. Murphy recovered from his gunshot wound and ultimately both amateur stage robbers were sentenced to prison.

Black Bart certainly displayed more intelligence and exercised greater caution than the run-of-the-mill stage coach bandit that Wells Fargo was used to dealing with. The very fact that his career of outlawry extended over a period of eight years attests to that.

To Bart's favor, he never drank to excess, never bragged or spoke to anyone of his exploits, nor drew undue attention to himself. His guise as a successful mine owner provided him the perfect cover, for it allowed him to absent himself from the city for various periods of time without being questioned by friends.

But Bart also was just plain lucky. His entry into the profession of stage robbery could have ended in its first attempt had not stage owner John Olive, riding inside the stage that morning on Funk Hill, prevented the young Sonora miner from bringing his Navy Colt revolver into play. With an unloaded shotgun in his hands, Bart would have been an easy target. Even if the Henry rifle which he was said to be carrying over his shoulder on a sling had been loaded, he would have had little chance to use it. His career also might well have ended in its second episode had not Mendocino County Sheriff J. R. Moore, as good a woodsman as Black Bart and an excellent tracker, remained on the elusive bandit's trail for a few more miles. Had he done so, the sheriff might well have come up on the sleeping bandit rolled up in his blanket and thus ended the Black Bart saga before it really got started. Bart, of course, was again unarmed except for the unloaded shotgun. Luck simply was with him that day.

And, although Black Bart made it a practice not to pick on stages that carried shotgun messengers riding the box beside the stage driver, he could easily have stopped a stage with a guard riding inside and have taken a load of buckshot for his trouble.

*   *   *

What the famed Concord stagecoach was to Easterners on the turnpikes along the Atlantic Seaboard or to travelers heading west on transcontinental routes, the "mud wagon" was to mountain and foothill inhabitants in California and Oregon. Although the Concords, built in New England by Abbott, Downing and Company, rightfully earned their place among the legends of the West, they were not as numerous on the West Coast's foothill roads as the lighter, somewhat smaller mud wagons manufactured by outfits such as Henderson Coach Company of Stockton.[5]

The first Concord stage on the Pacific Coast, after a voyage around the Horn, arrived in San Francisco in 1850, consigned to the California Stage Company. It cost $1,500 when it rolled out of the shop in Concord, Massachusetts, but it had to be taken apart again for shipment. By the time it was reassembled in California and shipping charges were paid, along with the cost of harness and six horses to pull it, the California Stage Company had paid nearly five thousand dollars.

The Concord would haul up to fifteen passengers–that included those who rode on top–along with their baggage. But it was a heavy vehicle and required the power of a six-horse team to pull it. Abbott and Downing used the hides of eight steers to provide the leather for braces, boot, and the suspension of a single Concord stage on its chassis.

The Concords were used almost exclusively by Wells Fargo for its intercontinental travel and also by Butterfield Lines along its southern route. They also were used on major valley roads in California and other western states. But on mountain and foothill roads of the Mother Lode, as well as in Nevada, Oregon and throughout most of the mountainous regions of the west, the mud wagons built by Henderson and others were the coaches of common use.

Well-loaded with passengers and luggage, a six-horse Abbot &
Downing-built Concord stage labors up an Amador County grade
in a cloud of dust. Stage travel in the gold country among other
things, was a hot and dusty business in summer and cold and muddy
in winter. The Concords could haul a dozen or more passengers.
(Photo courtesy of Amador County Archives.)

The mud wagon, itself a very sturdy and well built vehicle, was smaller and lighter and yet would haul as many as a dozen passengers. What was important is that it cost considerably less and could be easily pulled at a good pace by only four horses. Another of the real advantages of the mud wagon over the Concord stage, and the one that coined its name, was its ability to travel easier and better in mud, sand or snow. Besides being several hundred pounds lighter than the 2,000-pound Concord, the Henderson mud wagon's iron tires were a full three inches wide, an inch more than those of the heavier Concord. The mud wagons, which at times were forced to travel truly terrible roads, did not mire down as did the heavier stages.

It was barely sunup and a chill breeze was riffling the surface of the Stanislaus River on the morning on November 3, 1883, when Reason McConnell halted his stage in front of the Reynolds Ferry Hotel. Inside the hotel, in the glow of kerosene lamps, McConnell could see people moving about. He noted with satisfaction that the ferry was tied up on his side of the river. That would save him several minutes of valuable time.

A door slammed and nineteen-year-old Jimmy Rolleri, whose mother, Olivia Antonini Rolleri, ran the hotel, came dashing down the hotel stairs with several letters in his hand.

"Good morning, Mac," he called, as he traded the letters for a bundle of mail for the hotel. Then, taking notice that the stage carried no passengers, young Rolleri paused before starting down the hill to operate the ferry.

"Mac, can I catch a ride up to the top of the hill with you? That last storm must have started pushing the deer down from the high country. Jim Baker stopped on his way to Sonora last evening and said he saw two big bucks up there on the flat above Yaqui Gulch. I'd like to get a shot at one of them–we could use the meat."

"Sure. Glad to give you a ride," replied McConnell. "Go drop off the mail and get your gun."

Jimmy ran back into the hotel and returned a moment later carrying a well-worn but serviceable .44 Henry rifle which he handed to McConnell before hurrying down to untie the ferry. Limping along behind Rolleri came rheumatic old Henry Requa, hanger-on at the hotel, who would return the ferry to the hotel side of the river after the stage had crossed.

The river crossing at this low-water time of the year was the work of only a few moments. As the stagecoach pulled ashore, Jimmy Rolleri also leaped from the raft, climbed up on the box beside McConnell and retrieved his rifle.

Reason E. McConnell, thirty-one, had been a stage driver for the best part of ten years. He had left the Nevada Stage Company's Sonora office in early morning darkness and today was traveling without a guard. He was happy to have Rolleri's company for at least part of the trip. McConnell had stopped at the Patterson Mine, near Tuttletown, where he had picked up 228 ounces–nineteen pounds–of amalgamated gold worth $4,200. The Wells Fargo strong box he carried also contained $500 in gold coin and $64 in raw gold. As a safety precaution, the box had been bolted to the stagecoach floor.[1]

With no passengers and a minimum of freight, the horses moved briskly from the river bottom up the steep narrow road. For forty-five minutes they climbed steadily, then, halfway up Funk Hill Grade, Jimmy Rolleri signaled McConnell to slow down.

"I'll get off here and work my way around the hill," he told McConnell. "I might jump a buck out of one of those draws up ahead, or maybe get a shot at one up there on the ridge where Baker saw those two yesterday. So, thanks, Mac, for the ride. I'll see you later." And with that, he jumped nimbly from the stage.

"Good luck," called the driver. "Save me a chunk of liver if you get a big one." He waved as the boy disappeared into the fringe of roadside oaks.

Their flanks heaving from exertion, the six-horse team continued up the grade for another thirty minutes. They were rounding the head of Yaqui Gulch, the ridge top within sight, when suddenly the lead horses snorted and reared in fright. As McConnell struggled to control them, a hooded figure, shotgun in hand, leaped into the road in front of them.

There was no mistaking who it was or what his intent. He wore a dirt-smudged duster and the same flour sack with eye holes cut in it that every stage driver had either seen or heard about for the past eight years. This was the same spot, exactly, where John Shine's stage had been robbed eight years earlier, on July 26, 1875. In fact, this bandit, McConnell realized, had been hiding behind

Reynolds Ferry on the Stanislaus River was a busy place for travelers and stage coaches between Sonora and Milton. This route, during the 1870's and 80's was a favorite of stage robbers. (Photo courtesy of Tuolumne County Archives.)

the same boulder where the stage robber had concealed himself in 1875.

With the shotgun pointed squarely at McConnell's chest, the gunman, in a deep, authoritative voice, told him to throw down the box.

"I can't," replied the driver. "It's bolted to the floor of the stage."

"Get off that stage. Come down here and unhitch your horses!" he was told.

McConnell, stalling for time, said the stages's brakes were bad and if he unhooked the horses, it would roll back down the hill.

"It won't roll if you put rocks behind the wheels," said the stage robber. "Now, climb off that stage and get some rocks!"

Biting his tongue and praying he was not pushing the bandit too far, McConnell asked, "Why don't you do it?"

Much to his surprise, the hooded man, keeping his shotgun trained on the driver, worked his way warily around the stage and then, holding the gun in one hand, picked up several large stones and blocked the wheels.

With his patience clearly wearing thin, the gunman again ordered McConnell to the ground to unhitch the horses. That time, McConnell

Twenty-one-year-old Jimmy Rolleri was instrumental in the arrest of Black Bart when he fired and slightly wounded the much sought bandit on Funk Hill in Calaveras County, during the commission of his final stage robbery on November 3, 1883. The Rolleri family still retains the fire damaged engraved silver name plate from the Winchester rifle presented by Wells Fargo & Company to Rolleri for his part in the capture. The rifle was destroyed in a fire that burned his mother's Angels Camp hotel. (Photo courtesy of Richard Rolleri.)

hastily complied. No one could ever justly accuse Reason McConnell of not being a brave man, but he was not a damned fool. He was to marry Miss Rebecca Bunds, eighteen, of Milton, on August 29 of the next year, and that was a date he intended to keep in good health. He gave the exasperated robber no further argument as he began leading the team of horses up the hill.

Warned the gunman, "If you don't want to get shot, don't come back or even look back in this direction for at least one hour."

The bandit wasted no time starting to work on the strong box. As he led his team up the road McConnell heard the robber hammering and prying on the metal box. Several times he stole backward glances but was unable to see the man, who apparently had crawled completely into the stagecoach.[2]

At the top of the ridge, some two hundred yards above the stage, McConnell, who had been walking faster than he realized, stopped to catch his breath. The horses, immediately taking advantage of the pause, dropped their heads and began to nibble the short blades of new grass the early fall rains had brought. Angry and still breathing hard, McConnell stood watching the horses wondering what to do next, when a movement far down the hillside caught his eye. It was Jimmy Rolleri, rifle in the crook of his arm, moving cautiously along an open swale of land. Unaware of what had transpired just moments earlier on the road above him, Jimmy was still deer hunting.

Quickly tying the team to a small oak tree, McConnell ran down the hill a short distance to where he could obtain a better view of the boy, who was still in sight some three hundred yards below him. Afraid to shout, McConnell began frantically to wave his hat. Rolleri moved on, traveling slowly, apparently watching the hillside in front of and below him. Then, just when it seemed he would disappear without seeing McConnell, he turned, looked up the hill, and spotted the stage driver waving wildly at him.

The boy paused, then began to climb the hill rapidly as McConnell beckoned him. Within minutes, Rolleri, breathing hard from his fast climb, was standing beside the stage driver. His first impression as he climbed the hill was that McConnell had seen a buck and was summoning him to shoot it. Quickly, the stage driver explained the situation, and in a moment he and the youth were moving rapidly but quietly down the hill toward the stage.

It was McConnell's intention to move up quickly to the stage-coach, catch the bandit unaware as he worked inside to open the metal box, and with Rolleri's rifle either take him prisoner, or if he resisted, kill him on the spot. But, at least a hundred yards still separated them from the stage when the bandit suddenly emerged from its open door and instantly caught sight of them. He turned, grabbed a sack which he slung over his shoulder, and began to run. McConnell, who was carrying the Henry rifle, threw it to his shoulder and fired, but the bullet only kicked up dust behind the running man. He levered in a second cartridge, fired and missed again.

"Here. Give it here. I won't miss!" Jimmy Rolleri grabbed the rifle from McConnell's hands. He shot just as the fleeing man reached the brush line. Through the haze of black powder smoke they saw the bandit stagger slightly as he disappeared.

Running to where they had last seen him, McConnell and Rolleri found a bundle of letters the stage robber had dropped where he entered the bushes. However, he apparently had managed to retain his grasp on the sack he was carrying. Several yards down the hill they saw several more pieces of mail scattered on the ground, and when they picked them up they found that some were spattered with fresh blood, confirming that Rolleri's bullet had not missed. McConnell was confident that the robbery had been committed by the man who called himself Black Bart, "the Po8."

"You know," exclaimed Rolleri as they stood there viewing the robbery scene. "I'll swear that's the same man who stayed at our hotel one night last week. Later, when questioned by authorities, Olivia Rolleri confirmed her son's remarks, vividly recalling the gray haired man who had come to the hotel a week or so before the robbery and inquired about stage schedules. Mrs. Rolleri's description fit that of the stage robber. And, although she had thought nothing of it at the time, the man had raised the suspicions of her daughters and old Henry Requa when he asked for a key to lock his room. In those days, few people in the Mother Lode saw any reason to lock their doors.

Upon arriving at Copperopolis, Reason McConnell reported the holdup, and within the hour an ad hoc posse of local citizens was galloping out of town. Before nightfall Calaveras County Sheriff Ben Thorn had reached the robbery scene, and Wells Fargo Detective Chief James Hume, notified by telegraph, was on his way. Before leaving his office in San Andreas, Sheriff Thorn asked San Joaquin County Sheriff Tom Cunningham and Tuolumne County Sheriff George McQuade to set up a watch for the fleeing bandit.

At the robbery site, despite earlier arrival of the volunteer possemen who had managed to obliterate most of the tracks and visual evidence, Thorn found the stage robber had left behind a wealth of clues. Below the road, the posse had picked up a size seven and a quarter black derby hat. Behind a large rock on the uphill side of the road, where the bandit had hidden while waiting for the stage, but where the volunteer lawmen had forgotten to look, Thorn found a travel-worn leather valise. In the traveling bag was a pair of field glasses, a belt, a razor, three soiled linen shirt cuffs, two paper sacks containing crackers and sugar, and two empty flour sacks. One of the flour sacks bore the label of Sperry Mills, of Stockton, and the other one carried the name of a Sonora company.[3]

The sheriff also found in the bag an old handkerchief in which was knotted a handful of buckshot. What the significance of the buckshot in the handkerchief was, Sheriff Thorn could not determine. The shotgun which the bandit known as Black Bart used during his robberies had always been described by his victims as a breech-loader. For what purpose the stage robber might be carrying loose buckshot, Thorn was unable to fathom.

Whatever the purpose of the buckshot might have been, the importance of the shot itself quickly faded when the sheriff, back in his office the next day, untied the handkerchief containing the lead pellets. It was not the round, gray pieces of shot that tumbled onto his desk that caught his attention but the handkerchief itself. There, in one corner of the soiled cloth, Sheriff Thorn made out faded lettering. It was not a name, and at first the scribbling seemed to make no sense. Then the sheriff realized that the letters and figures at which he was staring– "F.X.O.7"–constituted a laundry mark.

Later in the day, when Jim Hume arrived from San Francisco, they reviewed the evidence found at the robbery scene, and

James B. Hume, former El Dorado County sheriff, for 31 years headed Wells Fargo's force of special agents and proved the nemesis of countless stage robbers, including the notorious Black Bart. Considered among the best of California's law enforcement officers, he was noted for his intelligence and fair mindedness.
(Photo courtesy of Wells Fargo and Calaveras County Archives.)

Thorn turned over the handkerchief, hat and other articles to Hume. The next day they talked to Mrs. J. G. Crawford, who had sold the bags of sugar and crackers found in the leather valise. Determining who had made the sale was one of the detectives' easier tasks, for, as her only means of advertising, Mrs. Crawford stamped the name of her Angels Camp store on all of her paper bags. The sale, she said, had been made the previous week. Mrs. Crawford's description of the purchaser fitted perfectly with that of the man whom Hume and Thorn knew as Black Bart and the description given by Mrs. Rolleri.

The two law enforcement men took careful note of their increasing store of information, but they also learned that their quarry, at least for the present, had once again slipped through their fingers. The volunteer posse which Thorn had directed to scour the surrounding hills for further clues had ridden to the cabin of trapper Thoms P. Martin, about a mile from Funk Hill. Martin told them that on the day of the robbery a gray haired man with a small beard had come to his cabin and when asked where he was headed, said he was on his way to his home in Jackson. The man, according to the trapper, said he had been visiting a friend in Chinese Camp. But he also had raised Martin's suspicions when before leaving, he asked directions to Jackson and whether he would have to pass through Angels Camp. Martin said after receiving directions on how to reach Jackson and avoid Angels Camp, his visitor left.

Thorn learned this was not simply a ploy used by the stage robber to throw off pursuers when a few days later he met up with "Doc" Sylvester, a local prospector, who said he had met a man in the Bear Mountain Range, south of San Andreas, who asked him how much farther it was to Jackson. Sylvester's description of the man matched the one given by Mrs. Crawford and the Rolleris.

* * *

Charles Bolton, as he preferred to be known, had arrived in the Mother Lode on this ill-destined trip during the latter days of October, 1883. In the foothills, October is one of the most pleasant times of the year. The heat of the summer has abated and winter's cold, rainy days are some weeks away. In normal years, the first fall rains have sprouted the grass, the oaks are turning russet, toyon berries are taking on their crimson hue, and in the deeper canyons, water maples have become pillars of golden flame.

Bolton had stopped in Tuttletown and, again passing himself off as a visiting mine owner, talked with the superintendent of the Patterson Mine. With little difficulty, he obtained a good idea of its weekly production, and from others he learned when its gold shipments were made. He walked the Sonora-Milton stage road from Tuttletown to the outskirts of Copperopolis. He also broke one of his almost iron-clad rules about being seen in public near the site of a planned stage robbery–he stayed overnight in the Reynolds Ferry Hotel.

On October 30, after considering several possible sites for his upcoming robbery of the Sonora-Milton stage, he chose exactly the same spot he had used during his first robbery eight years earlier, on July 26, 1875. He established a sleeping camp high on Funk Hill above the stage road where he could observe the flow of traffic without being seen. His meager camp, set up in the shelter of a large rock outcropping, consisted simply of a thick mat of dry grass over which he spread his blanket. At times he built a tiny fire to boil coffee. The fire was kept small to avoid any telltale trace of smoke. His only food was crackers and the sugar used in his coffee. In late evening he would walk nearly a mile to a spring to get water.

On the morning of November 3, Bolton moved down the hill in darkness to take up his post behind the same boulder he had used eight years before. It was an ideal spot for a holdup. The team of horses, after a long pull up the hill from the river, would be winded and traveling at a slow pace. In fact, almost in front of the rock behind which he was hidden, the road narrowed, going into an inside turn at the head of Yaqui Gulch, forcing the horses to go even slower.[4]

Keeping watch down the hill, he was gratified to see that the stage carried no passengers. Passengers only complicated things, like the damned fool woman who had flung her purse out to him. And, there was always the possibility of some idiot on the stage deciding to become a hero and taking a shot at him.

The actual stopping of the stage had gone smoothly–at least at first–except for the momentary argument with the driver about putting a rock behind the wheel. The shotgun had properly intimidated him, and as driver and horses started up the hill, Bolton had anticipated no further problem–except for opening the iron Wells Fargo box bolted to the floor of the stage. That always was a tough nut. And it always took too much time.

He was totally unaware of trouble as he dropped the poke of amalgam and the pouch of coins into his sack and prepared to step through the door of the coach. But even before his foot reached the ground he saw movement from the corner of his eye. Saw a man raising a rifle. He grabbed the sack and started to run. It seemed like forever before he heard the first shot. He heard the second bullet whistle past his ear before he actually heard the sound of the shot. He was entering the brush and thought he was safe when he heard a "thwack," like the sound of a windmill paddle breaking in a storm. There was a stinging in his hand, and the letters he had been holding scattered around his feet.

Bolton looked down, saw blood dripping from the ends of his fingers and dropped the other two or three letters still in his hand. He continued to run, carrying the sack containing his shotgun, the $550 in coins and nearly twenty pounds of amalgam, dodging through brush and trees for more than a quarter of a mile, until exhaustion forced him to halt.

Still breathing hard from his sprint, Bolton sank to his knees and gingerly inspected his wound to find that the heavy, lead slug had cut a shallow groove across the back of his left hand. Although the bullet seemed to have little more than broken the skin and was causing little pain, the wound continued to bleed profusely. To stem the flow of blood he wrapped his handkerchief tightly around the injured hand, then continued his flight.

Later, he told arresting officers, "I was so overcome with surprise and fatigue that a ten-year-old could have captured me." But he kept going. He found a rotten log, stuffed the amalgam under it and, a few miles later, hid the shotgun in a hollow stump. The only thing he kept was the $550 in gold coin.

Traveling toward Bear Mountain, Bolton accidentally wandered into Martin's cabin, got directions and headed northwest, not toward Angels Camp or San Andreas, but west of both communities. He probably crossed what is now Highway 12, somewhere between San Andreas and Valley Springs. En route, he found another cabin, from which he took a "fairly respectable" hat to replace his lost derby. By Monday night or Tuesday morning he was in Sacramento, having covered some eighty miles of Central California's roughest foothill country in three days.

His hand, although sore, had not become infected and was bothering him only slightly. He was more concerned about the appearance of his injury and the attention it might attract than about the actual wound itself.

On Tuesday morning he walked into a Sacramento barber shop for a shave and haircut. Then, from one of the town's better tailors, he ordered a suit of clothes. That afternoon he left for Reno on the eastbound train. He spent the next two or three days in Reno. While there, he wrote the owner of the Webb House, at 37 Second Street in San Francisco, where he lived, to say that he would be back in the city shortly. He also wrote to Thomas Ware, his laundry agent, telling him to hold his laundry.

On November 9 Charles Bolton rode the Southern Pacific back to Sacramento and picked up his new suit. The next day he returned to San Francisco. However, he did not immediately return to the Webb House. Instead, contacting no one, he spent the night in another hotel, where he was not known. The following day, when it appeared there was no danger of having been followed or identified, he returned to the Webb House to once again enjoy the good life.[5]

* * *

Notified on November 3 of another Black Bart robbery, Wells Fargo Superintendent J. J. Valentine was livid. Angry with Calaveras and Tuolumne county stage companies and with his own people for not providing guards for treasure shipments, he threatened to place an embargo on his company's acceptance of gold shipments in those counties.

The robbery of November 3, he noted, was the seventh Milton-bound stage to be robbed in two years. There had been fifteen robberies of Milton stages in little more than ten years, and the past two years had been the worst.

"If these robberies are not halted," he said, "Wells Fargo will be forced to place an embargo on express service to Milton as it has been forced to do in the El Dorado and Placer County towns of Michigan Bluff, Foresthill, Todds Valley, Greenwood and Cool in 1881."

Jim Hume returned to his San Francisco Wells Fargo office on the night of November 4. The next morning he spoke briefly with Superintendent Valentine, who seemed not overly impressed with the articles left by the fleeing bandit. Valentine was not interested in knickknacks found at the robbery scene. He wanted the robber. Hume then turned the evidence, including the laundry marked handkerchief, over to Detective Harry Morse, whom he had hired six months earlier for the specific purpose of working on the Black Bart case.

Harry Morse was no ordinary law enforcement man. He had served as sheriff of Alameda County for fourteen years and during those years had built up an enviable record of crime fighting. During the 1860's and '70's Morse brought law and order to the east bay area and to Alameda County. Almost single-handedly he wiped out Mexican outlaw gangs that had been preying on Alameda County and the Central Valley. He had broken up the vicious Narcisco Bojorques robbery gang and brought in outlaw gang leader Jesus Tejada, who out of pure blood lust, had wiped out all five occupants of a small Italian general store on the Mokelumne Hill-Stockton road. In a face-to-face gunfight, Morse killed brutal, bloodthirsty Juan Soto, considered the most fearsome of outlaw gang leaders in California during the 1860's. Many of the make-believe exploits of the half-mythical Joaquin Murieta were actually the bloody work of Soto.

But, in addition to his fearlessness and persistence, Harry Morse, at age forty-nine, in 1883, was a shrewd and careful law enforcement officer and detective.

For six months Harry Morse had met with nothing but frustration as he traveled the state seeking information that might reveal the identity or whereabouts of the bandit Black Bart. Now a smile of satisfaction lighted his face as James Hume laid the derby hat, handkerchief and other articles found at the Funk Hill robbery scene on the desk in front of him. Morse's grin widened even more when he saw the laundry mark on the corner of the bedraggled handkerchief.

"This," he told Hume, as he carefully inspected the bit of cloth with the India ink mark in the corner of it, "is the first solid clue we've come up with since I've been here. It won't be an easy job, but something good is going to come of this."

Morse wasted no time. He had no idea where the handkerchief had been laundered, but since he was already in San Francisco, he decided that was where he would start. A check of records at City Hall revealed ninety-one laundries in the city. It would be slow, methodical work without any guarantee of success, but Morse knew that was mostly what good detective work was made of.

For a solid week Morse wandered from laundry to laundry–from small hole-in-the-wall Chinese establishments to large company operations with several dozen employees. It was time con-

Tenacious and intelligent, ex-Alameda County Sheriff Harry Morse, engaged by Wells Fargo's Detective Chief James Hume, collared Black Bart after trailing him to a San Francisco tobacco shop.
(Photo courtesy of John Boessenecker.)

suming work, and if nothing else, hard on shoe leather. Then, on November 12, in Ferguson and Biggs' California Laundry at 113 Stevenson Street, the owners recognized the F.X.O.7 as their mark. Phineas Ferguson sent Morse to the tobacco shop of one of the laundry company's agents, Thomas C. Ware, at 316 Post Street.

Tobacco shops of the 1880's not only sold tobacco, but served as a sort of early-day convenience store, particularly for the masculine trade – single men and bachelors who lived alone. It was convenient to leave and pick up a bundle of laundry when a man stopped to buy cigars or pipe or chewing tobacco or other minor items needed in his daily life. The laundry, in turn sent a wagon there daily to pick up bags of dirty laundry and deliver clean ones. For tobacco shop proprietor Thomas Ware the operation of the laundry service ensured that his customers would come in regularly rather than randomly patronize the various tobacco shops in the area. Ware's shop was conveniently located on Bush Street, only a short distance from the popular Buckley Saloon, and men coming home from work often stopped at the saloon for a drink, then swung by Ware's shop to pick up their clean laundry.

It was late afternoon when Morse arrived at Ware's shop and learned from its friendly owner that the laundry mark, indeed, belonged to one of his customers. He was Charles E. Bolton, a mining man and a friend of his, Ware told Morse.

The quick thinking Morse introduced himself as Harry Hamilton and announced that he, too, was involved in mining and wished to meet Bolton. He said he had heard that Bolton left his laundry at Ware's shop and hoped through Ware a meeting could be arranged. Unsuspicious, Ware said he would be glad to oblige, and in fact, Bolton, who had returned from his mine only a day or two ago, should be dropping in at any time to pick up his laundry. Bolton, he added, lived in the Webb House, at 37 Second Street.

Morris thanked Ware, said he would return, took his leave and headed straight for the San Francisco police station. Captain Appleton W. Stone, friend of Morse and Hume, was glad to be of service to Wells Fargo and set up a stakeout for Bolton at the hotel.

Morse then walked back to talk to the tobacconist and at that time asked Ware if he could spare a few minutes to walk to the hotel and introduce him to Bolton. Ware agreed and, after locking his shop, started down the street with the detective. They had gone less than a block when suddenly they met Charles Bolton face-to-face, headed for the tobacco shop.[1]

"He spoke to me before I noticed him," Ware recalled. "I introduced him to the man I knew as Hamilton, and after they talked a few minutes they turned and went back down the street and I went back to my shop. I had no idea I had been a party to the springing of a trap."

Later, after he was criticized by some for turning "stool pigeon," Ware wrote an angry letter to local newspapers excoriating Wells Fargo for "using him" in the capture of Charles Bolton, whom he learned to his complete amazement, was the bandit Black Bart.[2]

When Morse met Charles Boles, alias Charles E. Bolton, alias Black Bart on Post Street in the heart of cosmopolitan San Francisco, he had nothing of the appearance of a stage robber.

Said Morse, "He was elegantly dressed, carried a cane, wore a natty little derby hat, a diamond pin with a large diamond on his little finger and a heavy gold watch and chain. Yet, beneath the finery was a man who fit almost exactly, the description of the stage bandit which James Hume had put together from his many sources."

This man was about five feet eight inches tall, broad shouldered, with high cheek bones and striking blue eyes. He carried himself with an almost military bearing, and his gray hair, receding at the temples, added to his appearance of gentlemanly affluence. Clean shaven except for a handsome gray mustache and a small imperial beard, he looked for all the world like a prosperous businessman, and yet, at the same time, Morse was just as sure as he was standing there that he was staring at the man who had committed California's longest string of stage robberies.

The fellow introduced as Bolton was polite and friendly and seemed genuinely interested in the fact that "Mr. Hamilton" also was a mining man. When asked if he could spare a few minutes to accompany Hamilton to discuss a mining matter, Mr. Bolton said he could. The two men, whom anyone, with the possible exception of James Hume, would have taken for a couple of successful business associates, made their way through downtown San Francisco, along Bush, Montgomery and California streets to Sansome Street.

Harry Morse glanced at his companion, who seemed completely at ease. Even when they turned into the doorway of the office of Wells Fargo & Company, this man who called himself Charles Bolton appeared undisturbed. Morse steered his guest to the superintendent's office on the second floor and asked him to sit down. A few minutes later, Charles Bolton was being introduced to his nemesis, James B. Hume.

Hume was polite and courteous. He was glad to meet Mr. Bolton, interested in the fact that he was a mine owner. Perhaps Wells Fargo at one time or another had transported treasure for him from his mine. Where was his mine? What was its name? Their suspected bandit still showed no apparent loss of composure, but as Hume's questions came faster and seemed more pointed, the answers became a bit more vague and evasive. Hume and Morse noticed beads of sweat on their guest's forehead.

At first, the man who called himself Bolton indicated that his mine was in the Mother Lode, then he told Hume and Morse they must have misunderstood him. His mine, which produced more silver than gold, was on the eastern side of the Sierra, near the California-Nevada line. Pressed for more definite answers, Bolton refused, taking refuge in the fact that he did not know what this was all about and that his mine was in a location difficult to describe. He also remarked that as a gentleman, he resented this persistent questioning. Hume and Morse continued to be courteous and careful not to anger their man. "If you would just answer a few more questions . . . It is quite important . . ." Then they would tell him what this was all about.

For three hours they questioned Bolton, and as their questions continued, his answers became more confused. He sometimes found he was contradicting himself, and this angered him.

They noticed that their suspect had lost a strip of skin; what might be termed a shallow gash ran along the top of a knuckle on his left hand. They thought of the bloodstained envelopes at the robbery scene.

"How did you injure your hand?" Hume asked. Bolton replied that he had hurt it while getting off a train during a recent trip to Truckee. Hume continued to be polite. "Is your mine near there?" For the first time, this man who they now were sure was Black Bart, lost his complacence. Angrily, he informed them that he was a gentleman and refused to be subjected to any further embarrassment. He would answer no more questions.

"What is wrong? Have you something to hide?" asked the detectives. "Certainly a responsible citizen and businessman such as you should have no reason for concealing the location of his mine."

It was becoming late in the evening, but there was no rest for any of them. James Hume sent for Captain Stone, and when he arrived, Hume, Morse, Stone and their suspect went to the Webb House. There, in room 40, the one occupied by Charles Bolton, they stumbled onto a treasure-trove of evidence.

Within the neatly kept room the lawmen found several suits, including a rough set of clothes that matched those worn by the man who had committed the robbery of November 3. In a bundle of dirty laundry was clothing, including another handkerchief and shirt cuffs that bore the laundry mark F.X.O.7. They also found a partially written letter which appeared to be in the same hand as the verses of doggerel found at the early Black Bart robbery scenes.

Lesser men might have faltered. But, with the noose seemingly tightening about him, Black Bart still maintained he was Charles Bolton and laughed at the detectives. "Half the working men in this city have clothes like that," he said, pointing to his traveling clothes which had been described by McConnell, young Rolleri and his mother, and others. As for the laundry marked handkerchief, "I could have lost that anywhere and someone could have picked it up."

James Hume agreed that a handkerchief can easily be lost and picked up by some other person. But the puzzling things about that particular handkerchief, he said, was that it was found at the recent robbery scene on Calaveras County's Funk Hill.

Feigning anger and indignation, the fellow who still maintained he was Charles Bolton, mining man, denied any knowledge of how a handkerchief bearing his laundry mark could have been found at a robbery scene. "Do you take me for a stage robber? I have never harmed anyone in my life, and now you stand there and bring my character into question."

Although he again professed indignation, it probably came as no surprise to their suspect when Hume calmly informed him they believed he was the stage robber known as Black Bart and was responsible for the November 3 stage robbery on Funk Hill. Black Bart simply stared at the two detectives and Captain Stone and held his silence. At that moment he had nothing more to say.[3]

By now it was midnight, and Morse, Hume and their suspect were exhausted. Hume asked Captain Stone to place the suspect under arrest, and a few minutes later he was being booked on a robbery charge at the San Francisco City Jail. Bolton continued his silence after being informed he was under arrest, but when the booking officer asked him his name, he replied, "T. Z. Spaulding." It was a name he apparently pulled out of the blue. He had never used it before, nor did he ever use it again.

One other thing that Hume and Morse had found in the robbery suspect's room was a Bible. It did much to clear up the question of his true identity. Penciled on a slip of paper stuck to its fly leaf were the following words: "This precious bible is presented to Charles E. Boles, First Sergeant, Company B, 116th Illinois Volunteer Infantry, by his wife as a New Year's gift. God gives us hearts to which His . . . faith to believe. Decator, Illinois, 1865."

Morris and Hume went home in the early morning hours, feeling they had turned in a fair day's work.

Black Bart had regained his composure by the time Morse, Hume and Stone arrived at the city jail the next morning. The Wells Fargo men and Stone had kept the arrest quiet, so there were no curious citizens or newspaper reporters waiting to catch a glimpse of or interview the state's most notorious stagecoach bandit. They informed Bart, who still pleasantly maintained that he was Charles Bolton and not Charles E. Boles or Black Bart, that he would accompany them to Calaveras County.

It appears that none of the participants in the unfolding drama had found much time for sleep. It had been well after midnight before any of them had gotten to bed, and they boarded the river boat headed for Stockton at 7:00 a.m. Bart officially was in the custody of Appleton Stone, but he was not handcuffed and seemed in a pleasant mood. He apparently still hoped that in one manner or another, he could avoid prosecution.

At Clinton, on the Alameda County side of the Bay, Hume's assistant, Jon Thacker, joined them, and Hume left the party to head into the southern San Joaquin Valley on other Wells Fargo business. Meanwhile, Morse had wired Sheriff Ben Thorn, asking him to meet their boat in Stockton and to bring the trapper Martin, who had given the suspected stage robber directions on the day of the holdup. It was Morse's hope that Martin would be able to identify the man who had asked him how to reach the town of Jackson while avoiding Angels Camp. Unknown to their prisoner, Morse also carried in his luggage the derby hat found at Funk Hill. The presentation of that piece of evidence to Black Bart would come later.

Although they had left San Francisco in anonymity, the situation differed drastically when they arrived in Stockton. Whether it was Ben Thorn or the Tuolumne County or San Joaquin County sheriff who let slip the information that a man suspected of being Black Bart had been arrested, now makes little difference. Word had gotten out, and there was a crowd, including several newspa-

The trusty's room in the Calaveras county jail, in San Andreas, appears today much the same as it did in November, 1883 when Black Bart, confessed there to his long string of stage robberies.
(Photo courtesy of Calaveras County Historical Society.)

per reporters, on hand at the Stockton boat landing when Bart and his captors arrived.

As requested, Sheriff Thorn had traveled from San Andreas to meet them, accompanied by Thoms P. Martin the trapper. However, Thorn remained in the background, keeping Martin with him until Morse, Thacker, Stone and their robbery suspect were off the boat, surrounded by a milling crowd of curious on-lookers and newsmen. Theatrically, Thorn began working his way forward with Martin, whom he then asked to pick out the man who had come to his cabin. Without hesitation, Martin pointed out Black Bart in the midst of the crowd of more than a hundred people. Thorn, Morse and Thacker were pleased with Martin's quick and positive identification. It would greatly strengthen their case when Black Bart came to trial.

81

Black Bart was incarcerated in this Calaveras County jail cell in 1883 while awaiting trial and transportation to San Quentin Prison. The jail, built in 1868, remained in use until replaced by a new jail and sheriff's office in 1963.
(Photo by Sharon Daniels.)

The newspaper reporters, mostly from Stockton and the foothills, continued to throw questions at Thorn, Stone and the Wells Fargo detectives. They knew they were onto a big story, and were making the most of it.

This was a period of extremely bitter competition between the San Francisco newspapers, particularly the *Examiner*, the *Chronicle* and the *Morning Call*. The foothill lawmen, in allowing news of Black Bart's arrest to break in towns like Stockton and San Andreas did Wells Fargo and particularly James Hume no favor. This action affronted all of the bay area papers, but chiefly the editors of the *San Francisco Examiner*.

Wells Fargo's people had run Black Bart to ground in San Francisco. They had found evidence linking him with robbery, they had secretly held him in the city jail, then spirited him out of the city without getting word to the local papers. When the story broke in hick town papers and the *Morning Call*–whose reporter had happened on it by chance, the *Examiner's* editors felt Jim Hume had deliberately allowed them to be scooped and never forgave him for it.

The enmity this situation created between Wells Fargo and the Hearst-owned *Examiner* took years to die. During those years the *Examiner* never missed an opportunity to discredit Hume and his company in the handling of every aspect of the Black Bart case.

With Martin's emphatic identification of him, Bart realized he was in serious trouble. He objected sharply to being photographed, but then his sense of humor returned and he joked about the danger of the flash gun. "Will that thing go off?" he asked. "I would like to go off myself."

He was photographed both seated and standing. Some of the photographs showed Bart in his most fashionable finery, wearing a salt and pepper jacket with its wide collar, complete with scarf and diamond pin. Another, certainly the most widely used photograph of the famous bandit, was a standing portrait. Clad in his well-cut overcoat, its velvet faced lapels open, derby hat set at a rakish angle and a polished malacca cane in hand, he fit the image of a successful man-about-town.

Black Bart was confined that night in Stockton's San Joaquin County Jail. Next morning, Morse, Thacker and Captain Stone rented a buggy and, with Black Bart, headed for Milton, in the western corner of Calaveras County. There, they were to meet stage driver Reason McConnell. News of their plan had preceded them, and what seemed like the town's entire population was on hand for their arrival. Wells Fargo detectives Morse and Thacker were somewhat disgruntled by the crowd, fearing it might make Black Bart uncooperative. Instead, their robbery suspect seemed pleased. He grinned and said, "Why look, the whole town's turned out to greet me."[4]

McConnell was waiting at the Wells Fargo office to have his look at the man who had been arrested. He knew it would not be easy to identify a man he had seen with only a flour sack over his head or, equally as bad, at a distance of a hundred yards over a set of rifle sights.

Confronted with the suspect, McConnell saw that this man was of about the same height and build as the man who had robbed him. But he said there was simply no way of being sure, for he had never really had a good look at the man's features. Then the detectives drew the two men closer together, introduced them and gave them a chance to exchange a few words. After a few moments' conversation, McConnell drew Morse aside. He was positive, he said, after hearing his voice, that this was the man who had robbed his stage on November 3.

That ended the Milton interview. The detectives with their prisoner headed for San Andreas, the Calaveras County seat, where Sheriff Thorn awaited them. Upon their arrival in San Andreas they found that again, a crowd of curiosity seekers had gathered. And to the amusement of his law enforcement companions, the crowd mistook Harry Morse for the robbery suspect and thought, for a few minutes, the well-dressed Black Bart was the Wells Fargo detective. In recording the incident in his report, Morse apparently did not think it was quite so funny, for he said he quickly informed the Calaveras citizens of their mistake. Jon Thacker remained in San Andreas only a short time, choosing to depart for San Francisco on the next stage, leaving Morse and Stone to continue questioning their prisoner.

By the time the lawmen reached San Andreas and had their prisoner lodged in a jail cell, it was getting quite late. They had been on the road some fourteen hours. Nevertheless, shortly after 7:00 p.m., Morse returned to the jail, and in the small anteroom that sometimes served as jail trusties' quarters, he renewed the questioning of the robbery suspect.

This time, the gloves were off. Morse intended to get tough, to pin down this man who he knew, in his own mind, was the bandit Black Bart. Morse had prepared a list of questions aimed at destroying Bart's defense. In addition, he had drafted in chronological order, an outline of facts that he hoped, presented logically to Black Bart, might force a confession.

Morse intended to hit this man with a collection of irrefutable evidence that would begin with Mrs. Crawford's identification of him when he bought sugar and crackers in her Angels Camp store. He would bring up the matter of Black Bart's wounded knuckle, the bloody envelopes found at the robbery scene, and trapper Martin's positive identification of him. No one had yet mentioned to Bart that the prospector "Doc" Sylvester had told them about seeing him on Bear Mountain the day of the robbery. There also was the matter of the letter found in his room which matched the writing on the verses left at the Point Arena-Duncan Mills and the Quincy-Oroville robbery scenes in 1877 and 1878. He also would remind his suspect of his stay at the Reynolds Ferry Hotel and the fact he had been positively identified by every member of the Rolleri family.

Midnight arrived and the questioning continued. Still maintaining his innocence and his identity as Charles Bolton, the prisoner alternated between pacing the small interview room and sitting silently, head down, elbows on knees, as Morse threw questions at him. At times he talked, always denying all knowledge of any stage robberies. Between Bible quotations, he talked of his gold mining experiences and reviewed his soldiering days during the Civil War. At other times he would discuss the evidence against him quite logically, then either switch subjects or accuse Wells Fargo and the sheriff of manufacturing evidence against him.

Morse tried to remain casual and keep from angering Black Bart, who still from time to time would profess anger that a "gentleman" could be subjected to such summary treatment.

It was nearing 1:00 a.m. when, after several minutes of silence, Bart looked at Morse and asked simply what if any good might come from a stage robber's decision to admit his crime. It was the first time his prisoner had even hinted of an admission to guilt. The first sign that he was weakening. Morse tried to hide his jubilation.

Calmly, the detective told the suspect that it might mean the difference between a reasonably short sentence and life imprisonment. "If a stage robber forced his accusers to take him to trial and he was found guilty of several robberies, a judge might well give him a maximum sentence," replied Morse. "On the other hand, if a stage robber pleaded guilty to a single crime with which he was charged, then went on to make restitution, that probably would be taken into consideration by the judge." Morse added that juries can be quite vindictive when they are considering verdicts against persons charged with multiple crimes. A judge, he said, considering a guilty plea, might be more fair minded.

"Suppose," asked Bart, "that a man who had committed robbery made a clean breast of the affair and made full restitution. Might he expect to escape a prison sentence?"

To his credit, Morse did not lie. "No," he replied. "The law does not look upon stage robbery lightly. A man who pleads guilty to robbery must expect a prison sentence. However," he added, "that would certainly be better than a trial and the possibility of spending the rest of his life behind bars."

Black Bart stood up and, for the first time, seemed truly perturbed. It was cool in the jail, but beads of sweat stood out on his forehead. He seemed to have forgotten all about the hypothetical stage bandit they had been discussing. His voice rising, he said, "I want you to know I am not going to San Quentin Prison! I'll die first!'

The conversation and the questions ranged back and forth, but always they returned to the possible benefits of confession and restitution of stolen loot. Behind it was Bart's fear of a lengthy prison sentence.

Finally, some time after 1:00 a.m., Morse arose, walked out of the cell and returned a few minutes later with Sheriff Thorn and Captain Stone. With all four men gathered in the small room, Morse matter-of-factly announced that their prisoner was ready to speak out–that he would lead them to the treasure taken from the Wells Fargo box.

It had not come easily, but finally, seeing the situation closing in on him, Bart decided on the lesser of the dangers facing him. He admitted the Funk Hill robbery. With Thorn and Stone in the cell, Bart stood up and said quite casually, "Well, let's go get it!"[5]

Thirty minutes later, with Black Bart seated between them, Morse and Captain Stone were in a rented hack headed for Funk Hill. It was a bright, moonlit night, and although it was mid-November, it was not unduly cold.

Perhaps it was his confession and the sudden lifting of the strain under which he had been for the past three days that loosened Bart's tongue. At any rate, he spared few details of his past several weeks' adventures. Then, apparently in the belief its statute of limitations had expired, he recounted the details of his first robbery at the same site.

Bart told them of visiting Tuttletown and the Patterson Mine. He walked the full length of the Sonora-Milton road, he said, and

In this Calaveras County courtroom Black Bart was sentenced to serve six years in prison for the November 3, 1883 robbery of the Sonora-Milton stage. Although the self-confessed bandit's true name was Charles E. Boles, he insisted upon pleading guilty and being sentenced under the name of Charles E. Bolton.
(Photo courtesy of Calaveras County Historical Society.)

chose the same robbery site he had used eight years earlier because "it still was the best holdup spot on the road."

Their prisoner also told them that one morning, while waiting for the stage to observe its schedule, he used his field glasses to watch another man wearing a scarf or cloth mask over his face, whom he suspected was also about to rob the stage. Bart said he toyed with the idea of allowing the man to rob the stage and then robbing him. "I thought that perhaps, if he got less than five hundred dollars from the robbery, I would turn him over to Wells Fargo and collect the reward for capturing him." But the man disappeared without robbing the stage, Bart said, and all his plans went for naught.

Bart also told them something of his life in San Francisco, of often eating at Pike's New York Restaurant on Kearney Street, near the main police station. He proudly admitted becoming friends with many of the police officers and expressed surprise that he had not met Captain Stone. He also brought up the subject of, on occasion, escorting quite respectable ladies, usually friends of friends, to the theater or to the city's better restaurants. Many of them were widows or relatives of friends, he said, who indicated they would not be adverse to closer relationships. However, he said he always declined to push these relationships beyond the point of casual friendship. "Think how shocked they would have been," he said, "had they known of my true identity and trade."[6]

Morse and Stone asked him how he had happened to choose the name of Black Bart. He explained that it had been the name of a character in a novel, "The Case of Summerfield," which had been printed some years earlier in the *Sacramento Union*. The leading character in the story, which had been written by San Francisco attorney William H. Rhodes under the pen name of Caxton, had been Bartholomew Graham. "This character also was known as Black Bart, and when I was casting around for a pseudonym, the name just popped into my mind."

He chuckled at the stir his verse had created when signed by the name "Black Bart."

It was breaking day when Black Bart led Morse and Stone to the brushy little basin down the ridge below Funk Hill Road. From beneath the rotten log over which he had hastily scraped dried leaves, Bart pulled out the sack of amalgamated gold. He told them how, frightened and exhausted, he had buried it, then discarded much else of what he was carrying.

He said he had retained the short barreled shotgun for several more miles, although he did not know why, since he had never carried it loaded, and in fact, had no ammunition for it. He finally took it apart, he said, and shoved it into an old stump hole. There has never been a report of the gun's being found.

They returned to the horse and buggy they had left tied beside the Funk Hill Road just in time to encounter the Sonora-Milton stage as it climbed the hill on its morning run. Once again, Reason McConnell had an opportunity to get a good look at Black Bart without his mask.

Back in San Andreas, Morse turned Black Bart, who still was using the name Charles Bolton, over to Sheriff Thorn. He then wired James Hume and Wells Fargo's division superintendent,

Calaveras County Superior Court Judge C. V. Gottschalk, considered one of Northern California's more learned and humanitarian jurists, on November 17, 1883, sentenced Black Bart to serve six years in San Quentin Prison.
(Photo courtesy of Calaveras County Historical Society.)

Leonard F. Rowell, that "Black Bart throws up the sponge. Stone, Thorn and myself have received the stolen treasure." Then he added a postscript, "Inform Thacker."

On November 16, in the Justice Court of Judge P. H. Kean in San Andreas, Charles E. Bolton entered a plea of "guilty" to the single charge of having robbed the Sonora-Milton stage on Funk Hill on November 3. He was bound over to the Calaveras County Superior Court for trial.

The following day, after waiving jury trial, Bolton pleaded guilty to the same robbery charge before Superior Judge C. V. Gottschalk. Although he openly admitted the robbery of the stage on Funk Hill, he emphatically denied he was the bandit Black Bart. Judge Gottschalk sentenced him to serve six years in San Quentin Prison.

The *Sonora Union Democrat* reported that when sentence was pronounced, Bolton smiled, glad the ordeal was over. The *Calaveras Weekly Citizen*, in reporting the court proceedings, said the prisoner "seemed rather pleased with the sentence."[7]

On Wednesday, November 21, 1883, just eighteen days after the Sonora-Milton stage robbery, Black Bart began serving his sentence in San Quentin Prison. Now in prison, he inexplicably insisted he was neither Black Bart or Charles Boles and that his name was Charles E. Bolton.

As it would turn out, due to recently enacted state legislation known as the Goodwin Act, which gave time off for good behavior, the man who was booked into San Quentin Prison would serve only slightly more than four years.

Court proceedings were brief on November 16, 1983 when Calaveras County Justice of the Peace P.H. Kean accepted the "guilty" plea of Charles E. Bolton, alias Black Bart, to a charge of Highway Robbery and bound him over to the superior court for sentencing. Bart refused to acknowledge that his true name was Charles E. Boles and served his prison sentence as Charles E. Bolton.

Lawmen of the gold rush days, like the outlaws they pursued, were tough hombres. They were advocates of "justice, swift and sure."

Although it would be neither truthful or proper to label them gunslingers, men like Wells Fargo's James Hume and Calaveras Sheriff Ben Thorn, if the situation arose, were not above "holding court in the street."

To be a lawman meant being handy with a gun, and the Colt revolver was his constant companion. But, when the need was for deadly, close range firepower–when the chips were down–most of the men who wore badges depended on the buckshot-loaded double barreled shotgun or the Winchester repeating rifle.

Police schools and academies were considerably more than half a century away. If a man was big enough and tough enough, if he found a sheriff or a marshal who needed a deputy, he suddenly was in law enforcement. It was strictly on-the-job training. And, in carrying out his duties as keeper of the peace, which sometimes included single-handedly tracking down and bringing in "wanted men," a lawman did what he had to do. There was no Miranda Decision. The sheriff of the 1870's and '80's didn't read arrested criminal suspects their rights. Crime suspects were not necessarily handled with kid gloves, and not to their credit, frontier officers sometimes resorted to various degrees of physical persuasion in extracting the truth from suspected criminals.

More than a few sheriff's deputies of that era were barely literate. Luckily, unlike today's lawmen, their job description didn't include the ability to write lengthy reports.

A good many of them interpreted the words "Dead or Alive" quite literally. They looked upon it as a hell of a lot less trouble to bring in a murderer, stage or bank robber draped across his saddle instead of riding in it. And it saved the county a lot of time and money.

But this was not so of James Hume or Sheriff Thorn, whose relentless pursuit put scores of criminals, including stagecoach robber Black Bart, behind bars.

Oddly enough, those two officers and Black Bart himself, central figures in that eight-year robbery saga, were all natives of rural New York State. They were all approximately the same age, all had better than average educations for their time, and all had come west during the start of the California gold rush.

Hume took up his law enforcement career as a young man during the 1850's, carrying it on into the Civil War period and beyond. During those times on more than one occasion, he was forced into gunplay. But Hume, an educated man with an acquired polish, relied on his skills of observation, organization and psychology rather than on gun powder while head of Wells Fargo's special officer force.

Born in 1827 in Delaware County, New York, to devout, church-going parents and raised on a farm there, Jim Hume was a scant three years older than Black Bart. When he was ten years old his family moved to Lagrange County, Indiana, north of the Pigeon River, and there he attended common school until age fourteen. During the following two winters, he attended Lagrange College Institute in nearby Ontario Township.

For the next seven years, while his older brother, John, founded a growing law practice in the Lagrange area, Jim worked as a partner with his father on the family ranch. However, by the start of 1850 the excitement of the California gold discovery reached Indiana and touched both Jim Hume and his brother

John. They headed for Saint Joseph, Missouri, and late August of that year found them mining near Hangtown (Placerville) in El Dorado County.

For the Humes, gold mining did not bring prosperity. After mining for a time they opened a successful general merchandise store in Placerville, but soon sold it. John then turned to the profession of law and was married. Jim Hume returned to mining.

From the dry diggings around Placerville, Jim Hume moved south to Columbia and Jamestown in Tuolumne County, but again his mining efforts met with no great success. The following year found him back in El Dorado County, eking out a living placer mining in the mountains near Grizzly Flat. There, in 1855, he first pinned on a deputy sheriff's badge.

Hume's initiation into the field of law enforcement involved no daring encounters with the criminal element. Sheriff E. B. Carson assigned him to collecting taxes, at that time part of a sheriff's duties. For his efforts, Hume was allowed to retain 15 percent of the taxes he collected.

Tax collecting was not easy. Residents of the gold country felt that on this new frontier, they had moved beyond the constraints of government. Most resentful of all were foreign miners subjected to an alien miners' tax of four dollars–one quarter of an ounce of gold–per month. The state legislature had enacted the tax on grounds that since the majority of foreigners owned no taxable property, they should pay the monthly fee as their share of supporting government. At one point, during the early 1850's, foreign miners in the southern Mother Lode threatened to take up arms in opposition to the tax.

Ignoring protests, Hume collected taxes and apparently carried out his duties with some degree of grace, for he was generally well liked by county residents. One reason he probably had less trouble than tax collectors in the southern mines was that the Placerville area had fewer people of foreign extraction. In early 1860 he gave up mining altogether to become deputy tax collector of El Dorado County. In 1862 he was appointed town marshal of Placerville, but still held his job as tax collector.

The town marshal's job included everything from catching dogs and criminals to riding herd on drunks and keeping the streets clean. Hume gained considerable stature when he arrested a gang of Chinese burglars who had been preying on Placerville merchants.

On March 4, 1864, El Dorado County Sheriff John Rogers appointed James Hume undersheriff. Within weeks, Hume received his first baptism by fire. Learning that three bandits, Ike McCollum, a man known as Scotch Tom and an unidentified man had escaped from Marysville jail and fled to El Dorado County, Hume took up their trail along with deputies John Van Eaton and Joe Staples. At Kelsey, only a few miles from Sutter's Mill, where James Marshall discovered gold in 1848, they raided an isolated camp and found Scotch Tom lying ill and abandoned by his companions. They lodged him in jail and two days later, just at dusk near Fiddletown, they unexpectedly rode up on McCollum and the other escapee, who took refuge in the brush.

Within minutes, more than two dozen shots were exchanged. Hume wounded McCollum, and the other officers believed the second escapee also was hit. The fight broke off when Van Eaton took a bullet in the thigh and Staples' horse was hit. The two fugitives escaped in the dark.

Two weeks later Deputy Staples was killed in a gunfight with a gang of Confederated States sympathizers who robbed a stage east of Placerville of its cargo of silver bars, at a place which ever after has been known as Bullion Bend. Jim Hume's unrelenting pursuit resulted in the arrest of all of the robbery gang except two, who escaped back to the Confederacy.

Another deadly gunfight in which Hume engaged occurred on August 2, 1867 at Lake Tahoe, not far from today's gambling casinos on the California-Nevada line. Early that day Hume received a message from Constable stage driver Charlie Watson that three men, headed toward Nevada, were robbing travelers on the Placerville-Carson City road. Riding at top speed, Hume and several deputies bypassed the three gunmen and just before dark arrived at Osgood's Toll House at the south end of the lake. There they met Charlie Watson and threw up a road block at the Echo Creek bridge.

Just before midnight the three gunmen, Hugh DeTell, Walter Sinclair and a man known only as Faust, all slightly drunk and in high spirits, rode onto the narrow bridge. Hume identified himself and ordered the outlaws to drop their guns. Instead, all three spun their horses around and began firing. A bullet inflicted a deep flesh wound in Hume's arm, but Faust was killed in that first exchange of shots.

Sinclair, slightly wounded, was thrown from his horse and captured. DeTell jumped or fell from the bridge into Echo Creek and escaped in the darkness. Before noon the next day, two El Dorado deputies who had been left at the American River bridge, east of Pacific House, caught DeTell as he rode back toward Placerville.

A year later, due no doubt to his many successes, James Hume was elected sheriff of El Dorado County.

During his years as a deputy and undersheriff, Hume had become well acquainted with lawmen throughout the Mother Lode. Among those he counted as friends was Calaveras County Sheriff Ben Thorn, elected to office the first time the same year as Hume. After they were elected, Hume and Thorn's friendship became even closer. On more than one occasion during the next decade they worked together to run down and arrest criminals ranging from horse thieves to stage robbers to murder suspects. Black Bart, in years to come, would also fall victim to their cooperation.

Ben Thorn had been born in Plattsburg, New York,[1] December 22, 1829, but when he was four years old his family moved to Illinois and he grew up in the frontier settlement of Ottawa. A farm boy, he attended local schools and apparently did well, for at age sixteen he was teaching school.

For at least three years young Thorn continued to impart knowledge to rural youngsters, but classroom routine suddenly seemed very dull to this adventuresome twenty-year-old who had just heard about gold being discovered in California. He quit his teaching job and joined a wagon train in the spring of 1849. September of that year found him mining gold on the Yuba River.

Unfortunately mining in the Yuba area did not prove too successful, and young Thorn moved south to the booming town of Mokelumne Hill in Calaveras County. After working there in what was known as the Rich Gulch diggings, Thorn again moved. This time he settled in wild, raucous San Antone Camp, on San Antonio Creek, in central Calaveras County.

Following James Marshal's discovery of gold in 1848, Mexi-

Calaveras County Sheriff Ben Thorn's sleuthing uncovered the evidence at the Funk Hill robbery scene which resulted in the arrest, a week later, of Black Bart. Thorn, considered one of the Mother lode's more successful lawmen, nevertheless became a controversial figure.
(Photo Courtesy of Calaveras County Archives.)

can and Chilean nationals were among the first foreigners to arrive in the California gold fields. They quickly staked out claims along the richer gold-bearing rivers and creeks and became bitterly indignant when in 1850, the foreign miners tax of $4 per month was invoked on all noncitizens—largely those of Hispanic heritage. The foreigners protested loudly, particularly the Chileans who were fiercely independent and felt they had as much right to mine freely as did Americans who arrived later. When a Chilean leader named Concha staked out a series of claims in the names of possibly nonexistent peons, fighting broke out between Americans and Chileans resulting in the deaths of two Americans and the hanging of three Chileans. Hard feelings persisted.

San Antonio Creek, rich in gold, quickly attracted a population that included Mexican, Italian, French and Chilean miners as well as people from almost every other corner of the world.

Quick tempered and resentful of the American presence, the Chileans, who constituted a large portion of the camp's populace, missed no opportunity to fight.

Young and tough, Thorn enjoyed the roisterous go-to-hell

atmosphere of the gold camp, but its uncontrolled violence and rising conflict between miners of various nationalities forced its inhabitants to remain constantly on guard. Claim jumping, arguments over gambling and the too few women, not to mention drunkenness, theft, robbery and murder at the hands of a growing criminal element, caused almost daily bloodshed.

One of the Ben Thorn legends, handed down from those days, deals with an argument between him and a Chilean miner, who, jealous over Thorn's attentions to a woman, drunkenly announced he "would take care of Thorn."

Thorn, who also had been drinking, reputedly wrapped himself in an American flag; then, singing the "Star Spangled Banner" at the top of his voice, paraded down the camp's main street, a Colt revolver in each hand. Whether his act was foolhardiness or bravery, it reportedly brought an end to the threat.

Owner of two claims which he worked with the help of hired miners, Thorn apparently made money, although he accumulated no great amount of wealth. However, with the acquisition of property, he apparently also began acquiring a sense of responsibility and an increasingly dim view of the lawlessness which was running rampant. He continued to mine his claims, but on several occasions during 1853 and 1854, he joined temporary sheriff's posses to help quell trouble and bring in accused criminals.

San Antone Camp at that time was largely a conglomeration of tents and clapboard shacks. Its narrow main street, ankle deep in dust and horse manure during summer and knee deep in mud and horse manure in winter, was flanked by saloons, gambling halls, fandango houses and a scattering of merchandise stores, boarding houses, livery stables and blacksmith shops. Few were the nights that there was not a cutting or shooting. Among the most notorious cutthroats was Pedro Ybarra, who would leave a trail of robbery and murder through central and northern California for fifteen years.[2]

On April 15, 1855, shortly after taking office, newly elected Sheriff Charles Clarke appointed Ben Thorn deputy sheriff, with the aim of bringing law and order to San Antone Camp. There was no shortage of ruffians and outlaws to start on. Thorn arrested some on various charges and ran others out of camp, and while he may not have turned San Antone into a model community, lawlessness sharply declined under his watchful eye.

Only a few weeks after pinning on his badge, Thorn faced down Big Sam Brown, the area's most notorious killer. Brown and a partner, while dealing cards in a neighboring camp, had stabbed two Chileans to death, wounded a third man, then shot another to death when a crowd of the dead men's friends threatened to attack them.

Thorn trailed Brown to a cabin several miles away. There, although the fugitive stood in the cabin door with a rifle trained on him, the deputy walked up and placed him under arrest. Brown served two years in San Quentin Prison, but shortly after his release was killed in Nevada by Minden area rancher Henry Van Sickle, whom Brown had threatened to kill.

Thorn, with a growing reputation as a peace officer and outlaw hunter, had a number of brushes with death and arrested numerous murderers, including John Phillips, who went to the gallows for the 1854 slaying of Mexican miner Juan Morales in San Antone Camp. He brought in Howard "Pike" Maupin for another San Antone Camp slaying in 1855, then traveled to Mariposa County, where during a gunfight he killed Santiago Molino –who had been accused of killing six men–when he resisted arrest.

Thorne continued to serve as a deputy sheriff throughout Sheriff Clarke's term, and following that as a deputy to Sheriff Bob Paul, from 1860 until 1864. Sheriff James Oliphant also kept Ben Thorn as a deputy, and he served under Oliphant until he himself became sheriff of Calaveras County in 1868.

In 1861, while being escorted to jail by Thorn, a condemned murderer, a giant of a man, grabbed Thorn and wrestled away his gun. With the revolver jabbing him in the ribs, Thorn grappled with the man and fought for his life. Before his assailant could cock and fire the gun, Thorn jammed his forefinger up the man's nostril as far as it would go. With a scream of pain the man dropped the gun and grabbed for the deputy's hand. Thorn then managed to throw him to the ground and hold him until help arrived.

Back in the fall of 1855 Thorn had been elected constable of San Antonio Township, a position which provided him revenue

Still a Mother Lode landmark, the Thorn Mansion in San Andreas housed Calaveras County Sheriff Ben Thorn and his family throughout the latter half of the nineteenth century. Many questioned how a county civil servant could afford to build and maintain such a pretentious dwelling.
(Photo by Sharon Daniels)

for serving legal papers. In Calaveras County as in others, sheriff's deputies also were deputy tax collectors. In Calaveras, they were allowed to keep as a commission 20 percent of the taxes they collected, including the foreign miners' tax.

Just how much tax money Ben Thorn collected between 1855 and October 30, 1859, when he married Anna Meeks of San Antone Camp, is not recorded. But, he moved his bride into a new, three-story brick mansion, the finest home in San Andreas at that time. Bricks for the pretentious dwelling, which still graces the San Andreas main street, were hauled fifty miles from Stockton.

The Thorn Mansion, as it quickly came to be known, contained thirteen elegantly furnished rooms, one of which housed a grand piano. Suspicious county citizens, including local newspaper editors, wondered openly how Thorn could build such a structure on a deputy sheriff's salary. It was implied that considerably more than 20 percent of the tax monies he collected must have stuck to Thorn's fingers.

In 1861 the position of tax collector was separated from that of sheriff. Thorn was elected tax collector and held that position through three two-year terms, until he was elected sheriff in 1868. During his campaign for sheriff he became the target of local newspapers which again suggested that he had embezzled tax funds. The *Calaveras Chronicle* pointed out that in San Andreas Township, which had 600 votes and $350,000 worth of taxable property, only $2,892 in taxes was reported collected, while Jenny Lind Township, with only 100 voters and $127,000 assessed valuation, had paid $2,900 in taxes.

The *Chronicle* also pointed to a shortage of $1,040 in poll tax receipts in San Andreas Township. Nevertheless, Ben Thorn was elected sheriff by a margin of 158 votes.

Thorn had other embarrassments. One night in 1875, Sheriff Thorn, thinking he was firing at a chicken thief in his back yard, wounded former County Supervisor A. H. Coulter, who was taking a shortcut home through Thorn's yard. The shooting cost Thorn reelection that year. However, he was by no means removed from the law enforcement picture. His friend James Hume, who in 1872 had become Wells Fargo Company's chief of detectives, often used Thorn during the next four years to help track down stage bandits.[3]

One of the 1875 stage robberies Thorn did not solve was the July 26 holdup on Funk Hill in which a bandit with a flour sack mask robbed John Shine's stage and escaped, leaving hardly a single clue.

Ben Thorn was reelected sheriff in 1879 and continued to serve until his retirement at the end of 1903. In 1883, he gathered the clues that led to the capture of Black Bart finally solving the mystery of the first Funk Hill robbery eight years before.

Although reelected for five consecutive terms, he never ceased to be a controversial figure.

By far the most controversial situation in which Thorn ever involved himself—one that shattered his friendship of thirty years with James Hume—had its beginning and end in neighboring Amador County.

On June 15, 1893, Wells Fargo messenger Mike Tovey, known from Calaveras County to Bodie and throughout the tough mining camps of western Nevada, was killed near Jackson by a highwayman's bullet. Tovey, a friend of both Ben Thorn and James Hume, was one of Wells Fargo's most trusted and well-liked men.

For nearly twenty years Wells Fargo messenger Mike Tovey's deadly shotgun protected the company's gold shipments along California-Nevada stage routes. Fatally shot in 1893 by an unidentified gunman while guarding a stage on the Ione-Jackson run, in Amador County, he lies in the Jackson Protestant Cemetery.
(Photo courtesy Calaveras County Historical Society.)

His death sent a shock wave through company and law enforcement circles from San Francisco to the Oregon border. Within weeks Sheriff Thorn had Tovey's suspected murderer in custody, but Jim Hume immediately voiced major doubts about his guilt.

The killing had occurred shortly before 5:00 p.m. as the Ione-Jackson stage, with five passengers and an express box aboard, neared the crest of Stoney Ridge, four miles west of Jackson. Stage driver Clint Radcliffe was at the reins, and Tovey, holding a shot-

101

gun, was seated beside him when a man stepped from behind a roadside tree and, without warning, raised a rifle and fired.

The bullet pierced Tovey's heart, killing him almost instantly. Frightened by the rifle report, the six-horse team broke into a gallop, nearly throwing Tovey from the coach. Radcliffe, holding the lines in one hand, managed with the help of passenger W. M. Shallenberger, also riding on top, to keep the dying messenger from falling.

The gunman remained beside the tree and continued firing. A bullet creased Radcliffe's shoulder, then the gunman turned his attention to the horses and fired twice more, wounding a horse with each shot. Despite their wounds, the horses ran more than a hundred yards before Radcliffe managed to bring them under control. The rifleman remained beside the tree until a buggy driven by C. A. Swain of Ione arrived. He then turned and walked down the hill into the cover of a grove of trees. Radcliffe turned the wounded horses into a nearby field, then continued into Jackson with his passengers, two of whom were women, and Tovey's body.[4]

Mike Tovey, a native of Canada, was about forty-five years old at the time of his death. He arrived in California's gold country around 1879 and, after a short stint in the mines, was hired in 1873 by Wells Fargo as a shotgun guard. Standing six feet six inches and weighing 230 pounds, "Big Mike" quickly established a reputation for fearlessness and calm, cool action in the face of emergency.

His shotgun thwarted several stage holdups and aided in the capture of more than one bandit. In 1879, with stage robberies on the increase around such mining camps as Virginia City, Bodie, Aurora and Candeleria, Wells Fargo moved Tovey and other trusted messengers from the Mother Lode to the east side of the Sierra.

Within weeks, Tovey was involved in a shoot-out on the Bodie-Aurora run in which he killed stage robber W. C. Jones, although he himself was badly wounded in the arm. Jones' partner, veteran holdup man Milton Sharp, escaped only to be arrested a few days later. During his trial, at which he was convicted and sentenced to twenty years in prison, Sharp vowed to avenge Jones' death.

As the mining boom along the California-Nevada border waned, Tovey was transferred back to the Mother Lode. On the morning of April 30, 1892, Mike was riding shotgun for stage driver Babe Raggio with the Sheep Ranch Mine payroll aboard, when a gunman, shooting from ambush, fired two blasts of buckshot into the stage. Fifteen-year-old Johanna Rodesino, a passenger, was killed, Raggio was critically wounded, and Tovey again was hit in the arm.

The bandit fled without any attempt to rob the stage. Sheriff Thorn was on the scene within the hour. He and C. W. Getchell and Getchell's son Clarence, who was later to become editor of the weekly *Calaveras Enterprise,* aided by a volunteer posse, scoured the country. Thorn followed the killer's track for most of the day but finally lost it.[5]

As soon as his wounded arm healed, Tovey returned to riding shotgun on Calaveras and Amador county stages. He was only a year from his own death, and it was during that period he received at least one warning that he was a marked man. Some months before his fatal shooting, Tovey reportedly showed a friend, W. W. Scott, a threatening note which had been left for him at a Jackson hotel. The note, enclosed in an envelope, had been handed to a hotel clerk for Tovey. Written in a scrawled hand were the words: "WARNING! If you want to live, quit Wells Fargo immediately, leave the state and never come back."

Tovey may have thought of the threat made against him long ago in Bodie by Milton Sharp, but more likely simply regarded it as the work of a crank. At any rate, he took no heed of the warning and, in fact, there is no evidence the note was in any way connected with his slaying.

His death on June 15 stirred law enforcement agencies into instant action. Within twenty-four hours James Hume and Jonathan Thacker arrived in Jackson from San Francisco.

Sharp, who by then had been released from prison, became an immediate suspect. He was picked up in Tehama County for questioning, but reliable sources convinced Hume that Sharp had been in Red Bluff, 150 miles from Jackson, at the time of Tovey's death.

Hume, by the end of July, was at a dead end for new leads in the search for Mike's killer. He had questioned and discarded several suspects, including former stage robber and ex-convict John Marshall, whom he found at Mud Springs.

Then on July 12 Sheriff Ben Thorn arrested a man named William Evans at Frank Rooks' ranch, near Cat Camp, on the Mokelumne River, and charged him with Mike Tovey's murder.

Evans, small, apparently easily intimidated and not overly bright, was lodged in Calaveras County Jail, although the murder had occurred in Amador County. He already had a criminal record, having served two terms in state prison for burglary. He most recently had walked away from the state asylum for the insane in Stockton, but since he was considered harmless, no one had bothered to return him.

On August 1, Sheriff Thorn announced that Evans had confessed to the Tovey slaying. And, speaking in the bay area as a Wells Fargo employee, Jon Thacker said, "We have been working on him for three weeks and I think we have the right man." Actually, Thacker had not even talked to Evans. Above all, he was not speaking for Wells Fargo and certainly not for James Hume.

Hume believed Evans innocent. He had met with Thorn during the hunt for Evans and at that time expressed doubts about the man's guilt. He told Thorn he already had checked on Evans, "and I know he is not the man. I questioned Frank and Lou Rooks, who are friends of Evans, and found he was with them the day Tovey was killed."

Thorn refused to believe the Rookses and pointed out that Evans had been using the name of "Gordon" when he was arrested.

Although Hume admitted Evans was no shining character, "he is a petty larceny thief, pretty worthless all around, and his use of an assumed name will work against him at his trial," the Wells Fargo detective chief still maintained Evans was innocent of the Tovey murder.

Hume pointed out that Evans' confession, which had taken several weeks for Thorn to drag out of him, could have been made by anyone who was asked enough leading questions. He was not surprised when, on August 8, before start of his trial, Evans repudiated his confession. Amador County District Attorney Richard Rust told Hume at that time that he, too, felt Evans was innocent.[6]

Nevertheless, as October arrived, the district attorney prepared to try Evans for the first degree murder of Mike Tovey. Jim Hume was affronted. During a bitter argument with Rust, Hume told him, "I will not stand by and see an innocent man railroaded to the gallows."

When the trial opened in Jackson, Hume was seated at the defense table and instantly incurred the wrath of prosecutor Rust. Rust asked sarcastically if Hume had appointed himself assistant defense counsel. When Hume attempted to answer, Judge F. D. Davis silenced him. He informed Hume that only an attorney was allowed to address the court. Defense lawyer Divol B. Spagnoli offered to address the court on Hume's behalf, but angry and embarrassed, Hume left the courtroom and returned to San Francisco.

Back in San Francisco, a still angry James Hume departed from ordinary procedure and chose to "try the case in the newspapers." On October 25 he told newspaper reporters in that city that Sheriff Thorn had obtained Evans' confession by plying him with opium and whiskey. After bringing a blacksmith into Evans' cell to rivet leg irons on him, the sheriff provided him with all the whiskey and opium he wanted, even though Evans had not previously been an opium user. Thorn also used a fellow prisoner to try to pump Evans for incriminating information. When that failed, said Hume, Thorn brought in Constable Christopher F. Masterson, posing as a jailed wood chopper, to try to get Evans to talk. Then, according to the Wells Fargo detective, Thorn forged a letter from Lou Rooks and showed Evans faked clippings from the Amador newspaper to convince him the Rookses had named him as Tovey's killer.

Drunk and angry at Frank and Lou Rooks, believing they had implicated him in a crime he had not committed, Evans, according to Hume, confessed the murder in order to drag them into the case. He said Thorn had assured Evans that if he would sign the confession he would never hang.

"I am not taking Evans' word for this," Hume told reporters from the *San Francisco Examiner, Chronicle* and the *Call.* "The sheriff told me these facts himself, and seemed very proud of them as specimens of the sharp work he had done to get the confession. I was, of course, much surprised when I heard that Evans had confessed the murder. However, when I learned how the confession was obtained, I was sure there was no truth to it."

Hume went on to accuse Thorn of offering the Rookses $500 if they would swear that Evans had not been at their home the day of Tovey's murder. He said when they refused, Thorn arrested them as accomplices in Tovey's death, but was forced to drop the charges for lack of evidence. District Attorney Rust, during the trial, admitted to jurors and the court that Thorn had offered the Rookses and other potential witnesses money for their testimony, but tried to cover it by saying he asked them "only for the truth."

One of the things that made Wells Fargo investigators sure the Evans' confession was false was a statement attributed to him that he had burned grass around the tree from where he allegedly had fired the shots, in order to hide his tracks. The grass, Hume told reporters, was burned by law enforcement officers after the shooting, in their search for spent cartridge cases from the slayer's rifle.

The trial opened October 16, and Judge John H. Davis threw out Evans' confession, declaring it "unreliable." Then, when two jurors became ill, he declared a mistrial. A new trial did not open until March, 1894.

The Rookses were among the few defense witnesses who testified on behalf of Evans. They said he had been hoeing corn on their ranch and was there at the time of the shooting. But, despite the testimony of Frank Rooks, his wife and their daughter, Annie, and facts brought out by Hume, on March 18 jurors required only three hours to find Evans guilty of the murder of Mike Tovey. Judge Davis sentenced him to life imprisonment.

James Hume was not surprised at the verdict. He had stated earlier he believed Evans would be found guilty, "since Sheriff Thorn is virtually conducting the prosecution and has a host of friends who will take his side in the case, while Evans has none."

Ben Thorn did not immediately answer Hume, but on May 25, 1894, in the *Calaveras Weekly Citizen,* he defended his actions and condemned Hume for his "low, contemptible cunning." He labeled Hume's charges "venomous lies" and said he never promised Evans he would not hang if he signed the confession.

However, he was forced to admit the other accusations, including sneaking the constable into Evans' cell, supplying Evans whiskey and opium, forging the Rookses' letter and drafting the false newspaper clippings. He defended himself by saying he gave Evans "only a little whiskey and opium."[7]

The rift between Thorn and Hume never healed. Eventually, the dispute ended in 1909 in a victory for Hume, but by that time both he and Thorn were dead. Thorn had died in 1905 and Hume in 1906.

In December, 1909, after Judge Davis declared that new evidence proved conclusively that Evans had been wrongly convicted, he was released from prison. Evans did not have long to enjoy his freedom. He was killed in a Los Angeles streetcar accident on March 23, 1910.

And, despite a search by Wells Fargo that continued for many years, the real slayer of shotgun messenger Mike Tovey was never found.

All that the whole episode ever proved was that although Ben Thorn may have been a very energetic man hunter, he also was a ruthless and vindictive one.

Just eighteen days after his arrest Black Bart began serving his six-year prison sentence. On October 21, 1883, Sheriff Ben Thorn delivered him to San Quentin Prison, where he was booked in as Charles Bolton, Inmate No. 11046. From the moment he stepped inside the prison gate, Bart became a model prisoner. Because of his exemplary conduct he would serve only four years and two months behind bars.

Why he insisted on retaining the name Charles Bolton instead of his true name, Charles E. Boles, he never explained. And, although he had not denied to detectives after admitting his long string of robberies that he indeed was Black Bart, officially on court and prison records he is shown as having committed only the single, November 3, 1883 robbery on Funk Hill.[1] Because of his obvious intelligence and education, not common commodities among prison inmates of the 1880's, Bart was assigned to the prison hospital. Quickly he became a trusted worker under the supervision of prison physician Dr. Rich and pharmacist Fred Fuller.

During his stay in the penitentiary Bart apparently developed few close associations with other prisoners, although he had no trouble and was generally accepted by the prison populace. One of the few with whom he appeared to have forged a friendship was tough stage robber and murderer Charles Dorsey, whose real name was Thorne. Dorsey, said to have been a former Confederate guerrilla who rode with Quantrill, was serving a life sentence for the 1879 slaying of Nevada City banker William F. Cummings.

Although there are tales that noted author-poet-playwright Joaquin Miller had ventured from his Oakland mansion known as "The Heights," to visit and interview Black Bart in San Quentin and that *San Francisco Examiner* reporter-novelist Ambrose Bierce also called upon him in prison, San Quentin officials said those claims were patently false. Other than a few newspaper reporters who interviewed him shortly after he was incarcerated there, Black Bart had not a single visitor during his four year stay in the prison, said San Quentin warden Shirly. The warden also denied the fantasies of writers who claimed that Black Bart held school classes for prisoners and taught Sunday School, stressing the importance of moral character.

No doubt, Bart did become interested to a degree in his work in the hospital and pharmacy as he gained the respect of both the prison doctor and its pharmacist. A *San Francisco Chronicle* reporter, in commenting on Black Bart's stay in San Quentin, said he had become sufficiently knowledgeable about the use of drugs and compounding prescriptions to take a position in a drug store. In fact, the writer of the article said Bart told him that he intended to seek a job as a drug clerk upon his release.

Black Bart, however, had hardly warmed his San Quentin cell when the *San Francisco Examiner* loosed a blast at Wells Fargo and James Hume, concerning the light sentence the stage robber had received. The *Examiner's* editors, apparently still rankled at being scooped on the Black Bart arrest story, accused Wells Fargo of obstructing justice in the interest of protecting its own bank account. The paper implied in emphatic terms that Wells Fargo had used its influence to obtain a light sentence for the stage bandit in return for his making restitution of robbery loot. Although he referred particularly to the gold taken in the November 3 robbery on Funk Hill, the writer insinuated that more than just the booty from the November 3 robbery was involved.

In its vitriolic editorial, the *Examiner* asked, "What is the result of this perversion of justice? A few detectives divide a few

The DeChamps stage (a mud wagon) ready for departure from the Union Hotel in Copperopolis. The driver is identified as Reason E. McConnell. Black Bart wrote McConnell from prison chiding him for having missed when he shot at Bart during the Funk Hill robbery.

thousand dollars and instill in the dime-novel charged heads of ten thousand youths of this city the idea that one has to be but a bold and successful robber to force the united detective talent of the coast to intercede with judges and obtain light sentences and get two-column notices in the papers . . . Whether Charles Bolton, who was recently sentenced, is Black Bart remains to be proved. If he is, then the law has been tampered with . . . The only tenable explanation," said the *Examiner,* "of such a miscarriage of justice is that Bart's prosecutors made a bargain with him whereby he received a light sentence and they, the $4,000 which he had hidden in the woods near Copperopolis."[2]

Wells Fargo and its detectives ignored the jabs, although other papers also were to take up the subject on their news pages and editorial columns. When Black Bart completed his sentence four years later, the *Sonora Union Democrat* renewed the charges of preferential treatment. The paper stated that Black Bart's short prison term "leads many to believe he made some kind of a compromise with the officers." Actually, it was an accusation that was difficult to defend. In relation to the average length of sentences handed out to convicted stage robbers during the 1870's and '80's, Black Bart would have to be described as a "short timer." Certainly, many highwaymen, with far less than the twenty-eight robberies that Black Bart had chalked up, received far more severe prison terms, and some, for lesser offenses, were sentenced to life imprisonment. Isador Pardillo drew twenty years in prison for a robbery of the Marysville-Downieville stage. Bill Miner, who robbed the San Andreas-Stockton stage, was sentenced to twenty-five years in San Quentin, and Milton Sharp served twenty years for the robbery of a stage on the Aurora run.

Bart had been in prison only a few months when he wrote to Reason B. McConnell, assuring the stage driver he held no hard feelings toward him. The letter, a copy of which fell into James Hume's hands, chided McConnell in a friendly manner concerning his marksmanship and showed that Bart had at least retained his sense of humor. The text of the letter said:

"You will please pardon me for this long delay in acknowledging your 'kind compliments' so hastily sent me on the 3rd of November last. But rest assured my dear sir, you are remembered with nothing but the most friendly feelings as a man having done your duty to your employer, yourself and your community at large.

"I have always admired your qualities as a driver and only regret that I am unable to compliment you on your marksmanship. However, it being lucky for me that I cannot.

"I would like to hear from you, my dear sir, if that is consistent with your wishes. You sir, have my best wishes for an unmolested, prosperous and happy drive through life.

"I am dear sir, yours in haste. B.B.

"P.S. But not in quite so much a hurry as on the former occasion."

Whether McConnell replied to the letter is not known. McConnell, after the November 3 stage robbery, also heard from Wells Fargo. He received $105 in cash for his part in breaking up the stage robbery and helping bring about the capture of Black Bart.

Nor was Jimmy Rolleri overlooked by Wells Fargo for his part in the affair. The company presented him with an engraved 44-40

111

caliber, Model 73 Winchester rifle of presentation grade known as a "One of One Hundred." The rifle was a beautiful piece of ordnance but for a reason no one ever determined, it literally blew apart in his hands the first time he fired it. Young Rolleri was unhurt, and Wells Fargo, upon being notified of what had happened, gave him a second brand new Winchester. The new rifle was of the same caliber and model, but it was a standard field grade. Inset on the rifle stock was an ornately scrolled silver platen which was engraved,

James Rolleri Jr.,
For Meritorious Service
November 3, 1883.

Jimmy Rolleri also was offered a job by Wells Fargo, presumably as a messenger, but his mother flatly refused to allow him to accept it.

Jimmy died in 1903, at age thirty-nine, but his sisters carefully preserved the keepsake rifle for many years after his death. It finally was lost in the autumn of 1938, when fire destroyed the

Main Street of Angels Camp was a busy thoroughfare during the period when Black Bart and other bandits were active in the stage robbery business. Bart purchased food there only days before his final stage robbery a few miles south of that city.
(Photo courtesy of Calaveras County Archives.)

Calaveras Hotel in Angels Camp, which his mother had operated for many years and which the family still owned at the time it burned.[3]

Again, at least in the Mother Lode region where Reason McConnell and Jimmy Rolleri were known, Wells Fargo came under criticism for what was regarded as its chintzy treatment of the two young men. Many Calaveras and Tuolumne county residents felt they were grossly under-rewarded for taking their lives in their hands by facing an armed stage robber.

There also was a lot of loose talk in the newspapers of the area concerning the supposedly huge reward which Wells Fargo agents were believed to have shared for the arrest and conviction of Black Bart. Such reports were totally without substance. Harry Morse did receive the $800 offered for the capture of the noted stage bandit. The money represented the $300 posted by Wells Fargo, plus another $300 offered by the state and $200 paid by the U.S. Postal authorities. Morse could accept the money because he was not a regular Wells Fargo employee. As in most cases where robbery loot was recovered, Morse also received one-fourth the value of the approximately five thousand dollars that Black Bart had taken from the express box in the November 3 Funk Hill robbery.

Because they were salaried employees, James Hume and Jonathan Thacker and other regular Wells Fargo detectives could not accept reward monies. However, Hume and Thacker were not forgotten–if only in a small way. An entry in the company's ledgers of 1883 lists "Mercantile Lunch, 2 dinners @ Black Bart, $18.75." Meals in those days were so cheap that two dollars in most fashionable eating places would provide a small banquet. For $18.75 the two detectives must have eaten well, indeed, as they celebrated the winding up of the Black Bart case.[4]

Thus, the rewards were handed out. And if the general public thought Wells Fargo's treatment of McConnell was less than generous in 1883, it was nothing to the outcry raised twenty years later when the veteran stage driver and guard was summarily fired for what company officials claimed was dereliction of duty.[5]

McConnell, who had quit stage driving in 1890 to become a Wells Fargo messenger, was riding shotgun on the Jackson-Ione stage when, on the morning of April 10, 1903, a gunman waiting

113

in ambush began firing at the passing stage. Loaded with several women and children, the stage was traveling rapidly downgrade and had already passed the gunman when his first bullet whistled over the heads of driver and guard.

McConnell was instantly on his feet, shotgun poised, but his view of the rifleman was obscured by the stagecoach itself. By the time he could clearly see the man who was shooting at them he was some sixty yards away–beyond effective buckshot range. Moreover, in order to fire at the gunman from the bouncing, swaying coach, McConnell would have had to shoot past the heads of the frightened, screaming passengers, subjecting them to danger from his own gun. He chose not to take the chance.

"Get the hell out of here!" McConnell shouted at the driver. With the horses at full gallop they were beyond the bandit's effective gun range in something less than a minute. A half hour later, the messenger and driver reported the attempted robbery to the Wells Fargo agent in Ione. A posse of local citizens left immediately for the scene of the shooting, which was not far from the spot where in 1899, McConnell had wounded one of a pair of stage robbers during an attempted holdup. However, the possemen found nothing but several empty rifle cartridges and a trampled spot in the grass where the gunman had waited for the stage. No trace of him was ever found, although the Amador County sheriff later that day brought in an expert tracker to try to follow the suspect.

McConnell, in his usual honest and methodical way, compiled a full report, omitting no detail, including the fact that in the interest of the safety of his passengers, he had not returned the bandit's fire. It was an admission that cost him his job. Wells Fargo had a virtually ironclad rule that its shotgun guards were to fire on any person who attempted to rob a stage carrying one of its express boxes. Company officials made no exception in McConnell's case, although his decision not to shoot had been in the interest of not endangering innocent lives.

Had James Hume been made immediately aware of McConnell's situation, its outcome might have been entirely different. He knew and respected McConnell's judgment as a driver and guard and was well aware of his coolness under fire. But Hume was a sick man, little more than a year from his death bed. Although he retained his title as Wells Fargo's detective chief, he had largely withdrawn from the company's day to day affairs.

Reason McConnell was fifty-nine years old, had driven stage for nearly twenty-five years and served as a Wells Fargo messenger for thirteen when the company let him go. During that nearly forty years of service he had been the victim of nine robberies or robbery attempts, including the Black Bart robbery of 1883. As a Wells Fargo messenger he had never lost an express box and during attempts to rob stages he was guarding he had shot two bandits. It required a brave man even to consider working as a stage driver or guard during those hectic days.

Three of the robberies McConnell experienced while driving stage occurred over little more than a two-month period during the 1870's when the Milton area of Calaveras County seemed to have a bandit lurking behind every bush.

On January 6, 1872, on the Mokelumne Hill-Milton road, a lone man armed with a large revolver emerged from the bushes to stop McConnell's stage and relieve him of the express box containing $2,900. Exactly two months later at exactly the same spot, the same gunman stopped McConnell again. For the second time, the bandit demanded the express box, but much to his disgust, that time it was empty. A week later, driving the same route, McConnell was asked by a passenger, Robert Lee Eproson, to show him where the two previous robberies had occurred.

"It's just around the bend, maybe he'll be waiting for us," McConnell jokingly replied. Moments later as the stage rounded the curve, driver and passenger spotted a man concealed in the low brush beside the road, a hundred yards ahead. McConnell jerked his team to a halt, and as he did, local rancher Alexander Wheat, riding horseback, caught up with them. With Eproson and Wheat remaining to watch the movements of the man hiding in the bushes, McConnell turned his stage around and drove back to the North America House, a nearby stage station, to seek help.

Within the hour a group of local citizens was searching the brush patch for the robbery suspect. He was captured after he broke from cover and was wounded in the arm during an exchange of shots with a youth named Jenkins, from the town of Jenny Lind.

115

The railhead town of Milton, in western Calaveras County, during the 1870's and 80's became the destination of stage coaches from all parts of the central Mother Lode. Both stages in Calaveras County that fell victim to Black Bart were headed for Milton when he robbed them. (Photo Courtesy of Calaveras County Historical Society.)

The gunman, to whom the local newspapers devoted a lengthy article but did not identify, pleaded guilty to the two previous stage robberies and was sentenced to prison.

The frequency of the Milton area robberies brought forth the following tongue-in-cheek comment from the editor of the *Calaveras Chronicle*: "The Milton stage has been robbed so frequently of late that the recurrence of this trifling incident has ceased to be the subject of comment. In fact, the stopping and robbery of this unfortunate vehicle has to be regarded as a matter of course and the omission of the crime creates more surprise than its commission. We don't credit the story, however, that the driver has become so accustomed to handing down the box at a particular point on the road that he frequently stops and sets it out on the wheel without being asked. That is gross libel."

McConnell also proved he was not afraid of gunfire, during the years he served as a Wells Fargo messenger. On February 7, 1889, while he was riding with Pete Podesto on the Jackson-Ione run, two men stepped from behind a rocky outcropping and began shooting at the stage with a rifle and a shotgun. Both Podesto and McConnell were peppered with shotgun pellets, but despite one disabled arm, McConnell returned fire and wounded one of the men. Podesto whipped his horses into a run, and the stage was not robbed.

116

McConnell and Podesto recovered from their wounds with no lasting effects. On March 23 an ex-convict identified as Fred Wilson was arrested in the Yolo County town of Woodland and charged with the attempted robbery of the Jackson-Ione stage. His arrest was brought about by the fact that he still bore unhealed wounds inflicted by buckshot from McConnell's shotgun. He refused to identify his partner. McConnell and Podesto each received a gold watch from the express company for averting the robbery.

Now, out of a job, McConnell returned to his home in Stockton, but he hardly had time to relax before job offers began arriving. Owners of stage lines in Amador, Calaveras, Tuolumne and San Joaquin counties came forward with offers of stage driving jobs. Within days McConnell was handling the "ribbons" for Joe Dechamps on the Calaveras and Tuolumne county stages. Wells Fargo officials must have found it somewhat paradoxical that the messenger they had fired a week earlier now was driving stages which hauled the express boxes he had been guarding. Once again, McConnell found himself driving the same stage over the same route on which, not too many years before, he had his encounter with Black Bart.

* * *

During eight years spent on the trail, James Hume had developed a grudging respect for the elusive Black Bart. Bart had demonstrated a cunning and intelligence far beyond that of any other stage bandits Hume had hunted down. Also, through use of surprise and a dominating stance, Bart had managed to pull off every one of his twenty-eight robberies without resorting to violence. It was something that even after his arrest, Bart took pride in. In fact, if he could be believed, so confident was Black Bart in his powers of intimidation that he had not even bothered to carry a loaded gun. That, in addition to his manners and way of life had set the "Po8" apart from his more violent and uncouth brethren who plied the stage robbery trade.

But James Hume, actually in private life somewhat shy and retiring, was a man of rigid moral standards. Following Black Bart's arrest, the *San Francisco Morning Call* began delving into Bart's personal background, and as a result, Hume's opinion of Charles E. Boles, alias Charles Bolton, alias Black Bart, suddenly plummeted.

117

Using information from Bart's Civil War records and bits and pieces gleaned from Hume and other detectives, the *Call's* reporters tracked down Mary Boles in Hannibal, Missouri. She had not heard from her husband since mid-1871 when he wrote to her for the last time from Silver Bow, Montana. She had sold her home, she told newsmen, to raise funds for what had been a fruitless search for her husband whom, by 1883 when they contacted her, she believed dead.

Mrs. Boles reportedly was eking out a living by sewing. Notified of her husband's situation and whereabouts, she chose not to come west, possibly due to lack of finances. Instead, she resumed their relationship through a constant flow of correspondence. Apparently willing to forgive more than a dozen years of abandonment, Mary Boles wrote regularly to her husband, looking forward eagerly to his return to Missouri upon completion of his prison term. Bart responded with letters which expressed his love for her and his daughters, and at one point, according to San Quentin officials, he wrote a scathing letter to his wife's brother-in-law, whom he accused of defrauding her of money. But as far as Jim Hume was concerned, the damage was done when he learned of Bart's desertion of his wife. Apparently, Hume could overlook stage robbery if it was cleverly carried out, but he could not forgive the abandonment of a family.

Hume, who had timidly courted his own wife, Lida, for five years before mustering the courage to propose, was affronted by Bart's callous treatment of his wife and children. His earlier respect for the holdup man vanished like a puff of smoke. His feelings, expressed to a *San Francisco Chronicle* reporter shortly before Bart was released from prison, were considerably less than complimentary.[6]

Asked if he felt the once-dapper bandit had been a cut above the run-of-the-mill criminals with whom he had dealt, Hume's reply was sharp and bitter. The question, as far as Hume was concerned, had struck a sore spot.

"In the popular mind," he replied, "Black Bart may be regarded as a Robin Hood who refused to rob the passengers or the poor and confined his attentions to the rich Wells Fargo Company. He is, in fact, the meanest, most pusillanimous thief in the entire catalogue. By his own statement his largest hauls came from the mail he always rifled, and from which he obtained more than

118

from the express. By doing so, he robbed the most needy–those who to save a small express charge, used the mail as a means of transmitting their money. From those poor people, Black Bart, boasting magnanimity, realized his largest revenues."

Said Hume, "When the express is robbed, Wells Fargo Company reimburses its shippers, but for the poor people who entrust their money to the United States Mail, in the event of robbery there is no redress. Their loss is irrevocable, for the government never repays them or makes the slightest effort to recover the money or discover the offender.

"Moreover," continued Hume, "aside from his criminal manner of obtaining a livelihood, his career has been entirely and completely despicable. The outlines were given to the press at the time of his arrest, but the details have only been learned since his imprisonment. Twenty years ago he left his wife and two daughters in the East and came West, first to Idaho and thence to Montana. From Montana, he dropped all communications with his family, substituting the name of Bolton for his true name of Boles, and during the ensuing 15 years, never sent one word to relieve the uncertainty of his faithful wife. While he dwelt in idleness and comfort on the proceeds of his crimes, she was left in poverty to endure all the misery of hope-deferred and heartbreaking uncertainty, striving continually to obtain some trace of him, living or dead, traveling for miles to see anyone coming from Montana, in the hope they might know something about her wanderer. And, when misfortune and disgrace made his whereabouts known to all the world, her devotion remained unshaken, as no one can doubt who reads the letters written by her to the heartless scoundrel in his well-merited prison cell. Whenever you feel carried away with admiration for the brilliant exploits of Black Bart, pause and reflect upon the sneaking and cowardly career of C. E. Boles."

Although the phrasing sounds a bit stiff, even for James B. Hume, and may well have been doctored up a bit and added to by the reporter who interviewed him, Hume's disdain for Black Bart's treatment of his family was apparent. Later William Randolph Hearst's *San Francisco Examiner* would use Hume's dislike for Black Bart to goad him into a series of heated outbursts against both the *Examiner* and the convicted bandit.

After serving only four years and two months[1] of a six-year sentence, Black Bart walked out of San Quentin Prison a free man on January 21, 1888. The stage legislature's recent passage of the "Goodwin Act," which allowed prison inmates time off for good behavior, had allowed prison officials to erase nearly one-third of this sentence. Bart had been a model prisoner. He had been helpful and willing in his work in the prison hospital, and apparently it was appreciated.

Present for his release were various representatives of the press, all eager to add some new twist to the Black Bart story. But no one else was there to greet him–certainly not Sheriff Ben Thorn or Jim Hume–nor any of his old San Francisco associates. Under a barrage of questions Charles Bolton, as he chose to be called, told the assembled scribes that his Black Bart days were over. He said he was older now, nearing fifty-five years of age, and could feel the added years. Not that prison life had hurt him, for he still was in good health, he said. But, he added, he was becoming a bit deaf and now needed glasses for reading.

He remarked on his work in the prison hospital and pharmacy, but did not bring up his earlier suggestion that he might seek a position as drug clerk. Bart somehow seemed more serious

COPY OF COURT MINUTES, SUPERIOR COURT,
CALAVERAS COUNTY, CALIFORNIA.

Saturday Nov. 17th, 1883,

Court met, pursuant to notice. Present Hon. C. V. Gottschalk,

Judge, W. T. Lewis, Esq. District Attorney, B. K. Thorn, Esq. Sheriff

and R. M. Redmond, Clerk.

THE PEOPLE etc.)
)
        vs.   )   INFORMATION FOR ROBBERY.
)
C. E. BOLTON,   )

Now comes the People by their Attorney W. T. Lewis, Esq. and
defendant without counsel, the District Attorney informs the Court
that defendant desires to plead guilty, the court thereupon asks
defendant if it is his true name, that by which he is informed against,
he answers that it is his true name. The Clerk under instructions of
the Court then proceeds to arraign defendant by reading to him the
information, and presenting him with a copy thereof, and is asked if
he desires to now plead to the information. Whereupon he duly enters
his plea of Guilty as charged in the information, and waiving time
asks the Court to then and there pronouce judgment against him, and
no legal cause appearing to the Court why sentence should not be
pronounced against defendant, thereupon the Court rendered its judgment.

THAT WHEREAS, the said C. E. Bolton had been duly convicted of
Robbery by his own confession; IT IS THEREFORE ORDERED, ADJUDGED AND
DECREED, that said C. E. Bolton be punished by imprisonment in the
State Prison of the State of California for the term of Six Years. The
defendant was then remanded to the custody of the Sheriff of this
County to be by him delivered to the proper office of the State Prison.

Book B. Superior Court Minutes, Page 76.

*As the above minutes attest, Calaveras County Superior Court Judge
C.V. Gottschalk sentenced Charles E. Bolton (Black Bart) to six
years in state prison for his November 3, 1883, stage robbery on
Funk Hill. But, due to newly enacted legislation which provided
time off for good behavior, Bart, a model prisoner, served little
more than four years before being released on January 21, 1888.*

than he had been four years earlier. When a *San Francisco Chronicle* reporter asked if he would consider returning to his ways as a highwayman, he indignantly replied that he was through with crime. Another reporter, also seeking to reopen the question of his past, asked if he would write more poetry. Bart turned on him with a mock frown. "Young man, didn't you just hear me say I would commit no more crimes?"[2]

There was some light banter as they waited for the boat at the prison wharf, but Bart answered few serious questions. He made no serious commitment concerning his future plans, nor did he speak of his family or of returning to the East to rejoin his wife. To his credit, he did not fall back on the weary old ploy of so many, who upon their release from prison, profess that while behind bars they found God and gave up their evil ways. He had not gotten religion. He did not ask forgiveness and he did not tell his interviewers he was a reformed man.

Remaining in San Francisco, Bart moved into the Nevada House at 132 Sixth Street, a small boarding house-hotel run by a Mrs. Burling. While he stayed there, Wells Fargo agents took quiet pains to keep track of him, but his movements appeared quite limited. Apparently he led an almost reclusive life, shunning all former friends and acquaintances.

Another question that remains unanswered concerning the period following his release from San Quentin is what Bart used for money. He had several hundred dollars in his possession when he was arrested following the November 3, 1883 Funk Hill robbery, but that undoubtedly was construed to be part of the robbery loot. It hardly seems conceivable that he would have been allowed to keep it or that it would have been returned to him following his release.

Was it possible that somewhere in San Francisco he had a hidden bank account or some money cached away?

On January 23, 1888, just two days after Bart's release from prison, a puzzling ad appeared in the "Personals" column of the *San Francisco Examiner*. The terse message, printed only once, stated: "Black Bart will hear something to his advantage by sending his address to M.R., Box 29, this office." Many persons saw the notice, and the fact it appeared in the paper only once made most believe that Bart had seen it too and immediately answered it.

Who might have placed the ad or to what it may have pertained remains a mystery. Some romantics guessed it might have been placed by a woman–possibly Bart's mythical mistress. Others thought it was the work of someone hoping to cash in on Bart's notoriety, while some students of Black Bart history think it was placed by the *Examiner* itself, simply in the hope of developing another story.

Whether anything came of the notice in the "Personals" column, or even whether Black Bart knew about it, remains unknown. About that time he turned down an offer of a theatrical engagement from the Oakwood Theater and Dietz Opera House. In a letter a few days later to his wife, Bart said, "I will not lend myself to any dime museum fiction."

Another thing that Black Bart did not do was return to his wife, Mary, in Hannibal, Missouri, where she was living with a married daughter. There is no question that they corresponded for some time after he was freed from prison, for Mary Boles later sent some letters to James Hume in the hope that he might persuade her husband to return to her. At least some of those letters were printed in bay area newspapers.[3]

One of Bart's letters that his wife sent to Hume indicated that at the very least he was indulging in a bit of self pity, or more than that, he was seeking an easy way of telling her he was not going to return. The letter was less than complimentary to the San Quentin Prison medical facility and its staff, with whom he had endured forced association for the past four years.

In his letter, Bart stated: "Dear Family: I am completely demoralized and feel like getting entirely out of the reach of everybody for a few months and see what effect that will have. Oh, my dear family, how little you know of the terrible ordeal I have passed through and what few of what the world calls good men are worth the giant powder it would take to blow them to eternity. Thousands that under your every day life you would call good, nice, men are–until the circumstances change to give them a chance to show their real character.

"I have reference now to those that have charge of our public institutions. For instance, you might go about them as a visitor and meet men there that you would think the very essence of official purity. But go into the hospital and see there what they

123

Charles E. Bolton's release papers from San Quentin Prison include his physical description that lists bullet scars on forehead and wrist received when fired at during stage robbery attempts, as well as a long-healed abdominal wound received in combat during the Civil War.

are doing for those who need their care and you fill find 99, yes 99 in every 100, that would not turn a hand to save a prisoner's life! . . ."

There is no evidence that Hume, who by now had lost all sympathy for Black Bart, ever made any effort to contact him personally or persuade him to return to his wife, other than turning one or more of her letters over to the newspapers. Bart apparently continued to answer his wife's letters, expressing affection and allowing her to hope he would return. A letter from her husband that Mary Boles forwarded to James Hume said: "All other relationships are like 'ropes of sand.' How I do hope you may retain your health until I can come home to you. I hope you will not think or attribute my not coming home to any lack of desire on my part or lack of affection for you. I do regret not being able to come to you. The clouds look dark and gloomy and the real struggle of life is at hand. I must meet it and fight it out. Let come what may, I must see my own loved Mary and our loving children once more. When that time comes, then and not until then, can I expect the first ray of sunlight to enter my poor, desolate, bleeding heart . . . ."

But despite continued flowery phrases Bart made no effort to return to his wife or daughters, who now were adults with families of their own. He continued to stay at the Nevada House, remaining largely out of contact with the world.

Bart's final letter to his wife, part of which she mailed to Detective Hume, still expressed love for her but was emphatic on one point. He was not coming home. It read:

"Oh, my constant loving Mary and children: I did hope and had good reason for hoping to be able to come to you and end all this terrible uncertainty but it seems it will end only in my life. Although I am "Free" and in fair health, I am most miserable. My dear family, I wish you would give me up forever and be happy, for I feel I will be a burden to you as I live, no matter where I am. My loving family, I would willingly sacrifice my life to enjoy your living company for a week as I once was. I fear you will blame me for not coming but Heaven knows it is an utter impossibility. I love you but I fear you will not believe me & I know the world will scoff at the idea."

The letter apparently was mailed in San Francisco, but, since Mary Boles sent only a portion of it to Hume, the date it was written is not known. Why her husband chose not to join her in Missouri remains simply another of the unanswered questions that surround the Black Bart saga. There can be little doubt that Mary Boles, living with a married daughter in Hannibal, was deeply disappointed by her husband's decision not to come home.

The *San Francisco Chronicle* reported that prior to Bart's release from prison, Mrs. Boles, in a letter to San Quentin's Captain Charles Aull, asked his advice as to whether she should come west to convince her husband of her love and that he should return to

Missouri with her. According to the paper, Aull told her the trip was unnecessary, since Bart already had announced plans to join her upon completion of his prison term. Apparently she accepted Aull's counsel, for by the time she learned from Bart that he had changed his mind, it was too late. He had left San Francisco and quietly slipped into oblivion.

* * *

Black Bart may have been remorseful about not returning to his family, but if he was remorseful about turning to a life of crime, he never expressed it. Rather, when talking to reporters or lawmen, he indicated a sort of pride in his ability to have eluded the law for so long a time. It also seemed, when questioned by reporters on the possibility of returning to his old ways, that his decision to abandon crime was based more on the fear of being caught again than on his rehabilitation and sorrow for his sins of the past.

Bart was not an egotistical man, but he was not one to humble himself. Even in prison he stood head and shoulders, both in deportment and general intelligence, above the average convict—seemingly more a peer of his captors than of his fellow prisoners.[4]

Upon his release from San Quentin Bart seemed, at least while in San Francisco, to withdraw unto himself. There were no reports of his being seen in his old haunts although there certainly were those who would have welcomed his return to their society and probably would have enjoyed basking in his notoriety. Instead, he apparently shunned former friends and acquaintances. After the initial spate of stories concerning his release from prison splashed across the front pages of California's newspapers, the press lost interest in him.

The ad in the *Examiner* the day after he was freed drew some speculation, but there was no way to trace the person who placed it. Bart's movements did not seem to have been affected or changed by it, at least during the period he remained in San Francisco. He might have had a bit of money stashed away, but it could not have been much. He had to see about making a living, lawfully or unlawfully, for it takes money to live.

James Hume professed little interest in the former stage bandit, although Wells Fargo & Company kept close tabs on him while he was at the Nevada House. Asked by a reporter if he feared Black Bart might return to stage robbery, Hume said he had not given it much thought. "I don't know or care very much because he won't remain in the holdup business very long if he does," replied Hume. "Every law enforcement officer in California and western Nevada has his photograph and we know his method of operation. He couldn't live in the woods very long and he never again could hide in San Francisco or even in the smallest mountain town. Charles Boles, call him Charles Bolton or Black Bart, if you wish, is too well known now."

Hume apparently could not resist casting at least a small barb at the press. "Maybe," he said, "some of his admirers may take him into business with them as a drawing card, or as you call it—a display ad."[5]

In truth, Hume probably was not too concerned about Black Bart's future plans. Stage robbery no longer was big business. The Wells Fargo express boxes the stages carried no longer contained rich treasure from the mines. In 1886, for instance, fifteen stage robberies had cost Wells Fargo considerably less than one thousand dollars. Of more importance to Wells Fargo and to Hume during the latter 1880's were the growing incidents of train robbery. Since November 4, 1870, when the Central Pacific's crack, eastbound passenger train was stopped near Verdi, Nevada, and $41,000 in gold coin was removed at gunpoint from its express car, train robbery had become a growing problem. That was the West's first train robbery, but by the 1880's railroad express cars had become the outlaws' favorite prey. The nationally-published *Express Gazette* reported that between 1890 and 1900, there were 290 train robberies across the nation, the majority of them occurring in the west.

So, if Jim Hume did not seem too concerned about Black Bart's freedom or his future plans, he had good reason. Train robbery, not some lone masked bandit on an isolated country road, was his major worry.

In Calaveras County, Sheriff Thorn, who by 1888 was indicating to friends it was he and not special officer Harry Morse who had extracted the confession from Black Bart, also made inquiries concerning Bart's whereabouts. However, neither Thorn

127

nor Hume appeared worried about Bart's possible return to crime. As Hume often said, during those years of the late '80's and during the '90's, "there just isn't enough profit in stage robbery any more to attract the first rate criminal."

In fact, it appears that most California lawmen, by 1888, believed that as a criminal, Black Bart was history. Even the handkerchief with its telltale laundry mark that led to his arrest had become a museum piece, on display under glass in a museum room that Sheriff Tom Cunningham had set up in his San Joaquin County Jail. Apparently, after Bart pleaded guilty to the robbery of the Sonora-Milton stage and had been sentenced to prison, Sheriff Thorn gave the handkerchief to his friend Cunningham to become a part of the museum display which has, unfortunately, long since disappeared.

The late John Ross, of Mountain Ranch in Calaveras County, whose mining career spanned some seventy years in California's Mother Lode and in Nevada, said that shortly after his release from prison, Black Bart revisited Calaveras County and stayed for a short time in Copperopolis. Ross, who early in this century served as superintendent of several major mining operations in Copperopolis, said he was told by numerous "old timers" of Bart's visit. What his business might have been, or how long he stayed, Ross did not know.

"They said there were some people here and in other places in the county who were pretty damned well worried when word got around that Black Bart was back," commented Ross. "Apparently they thought he had returned to even some old scores, but nothing happened and he left as quietly as he came."

To back up his statement that the former stage robber had come back to Calaveras, Ross, who in later life was editor and publisher of the *American Gold News*, produced a photograph of several persons on the porch of what appears to be a rooming house or hotel. One of the men in the photograph bore a remarkable likeness to the man known as Black Bart. Some current historians say the photograph is spurious. There really is no way of proving that the man in the picture is or isn't the person who called himself Charles Bolton.[6] There are other reports, some accompanied by relatively convincing evidence, that Black Bart was

During the latter months of 1888, residents of San Andreas, were more interested in the upcoming presidential election than in reports that Black Bart, recently released from prison, had returned to stage robbery. It was in the Calaveras County Courthouse on Main Street here, that Bart had been sentenced to six years in prison.

seen in Calaveras and other Mother Lode counties during the final years of the nineteenth century and early years of the twentieth century.

One of those reports emanates from Calaveras County's historic Murphys (then the Mitchler) Hotel. Mrs. Rose Schwoerer, member of a prominent Calaveras family, often recalled in later life that in 1909, when she was a girl waiting on tables in the hotel, owner Frank Mitchler quietly drew the attention of cook and waitresses to an elderly, partially bald man eating dinner in a corner of the dining room. That man, Mitchler informed them, was the notorious stage robber Black Bart.

Certainly, Black Bart was no stranger to the Murphys Hotel. He had stayed there on three occasions prior to his arrest for the Funk Hill stage robbery. On February 10, 1880, in handwriting that appears to be that of the man known as Black Bart, he registered as Carlos E. Bolton. Then, on February 11 and again on February 19 of that year, he registered as C. E. Bolton.[7]

There is no registration at the hotel for anyone named Bolton in 1909, but that does not mean that he could not have dined there. If in truth the man pointed out by Mitchler was Black Bart, he would have been seventy-six or seventy-seven years old. Certainly, Frank Mitchler would have been familiar with photographs of Black Bart, if not with the man himself. Mitchler would not have made his statement to the hotel help if he had not believed it, and Mrs. Schwoerer's word is above reproach. However, he could have been mistaken, and there is no reason to believe or disbelieve the diner actually was the former stage bandit. The incident remains simply another of the little Black Bart mysteries.

But this much is known. One day in February, 1888, Black Bart was in San Francisco, staying quietly at the Nevada House. The next day, without a trace, he was gone.

10

Black Bart had vanished. He simply was nowhere to be found. Bart had been well aware that he was being kept under surveillance and, not being naive, he was pretty sure–positive in fact–that the people keeping an eye on him at his shabby, Sixth Street boarding house-hotel were Wells Fargo agents.

Portions of a letter that Mary Boles sent to the James Hume about that time, as she sought to verify her husband's whereabouts, contained information that Bart knew he was being watched. He told his wife, "I have made no effort to avoid them, but when I do, Mr. Detective will find his hands full to keep track of me. Not that I care for anything, only the contemptible annoyance of his constant presence . . . "

Bart may have been piling it on a bit thick there, but also, he may well have worried that either Wells Fargo & Company or some law enforcement agency might try to frame him with another crime. He added, "I know too, if they can, they will put a job on me if I remain among them. They think that, I having served a term, it will be easy to fasten a second job on me. But I don't propose to allow them to succeed in anything they can concert against me.

"I am entirely demoralized and feel like getting entirely out of reach of everybody for a few months."

There was no way of telling when Bart had written the letter, for Mary Boles had not included the entire piece. Instead, she had merely snipped excerpts from it which she enclosed in her own letter to Hume. Probably, it was written in early February.

At any rate, some time in mid-February Black Bart was gone. Reports drifted in to Wells Fargo headquarters that he had been seen in Modesto, had stayed a few days in Merced, then traveled on to Madera. No doubt, Wells Fargo and possibly some law enforcement bodies made discreet inquiries as to his presence, but if they did their efforts were to no avail.

Then, some time in late March Hume received a letter and a parcel from the owner of the Palace Hotel in Visalia, California. The letter informed the detective chief that on February 28, 1888, a Mr. Moore had registered at his hostelry, then disappeared. The package contained a valise, and when he opened it, Hume found a can of corned beef, a can of tongue, a pound of coffee, packages of crackers and sugar, a jar of currant jelly, two neckties and two pairs of cuffs bearing the laundry mark F.X.O.7. Was the whole thing a plant by Black Bart simply to worry or aggravate Jim Hume? Perhaps it was a way of paying back Wells Fargo for its unwelcome surveillance after his release from prison. Had he planned a robbery in the Visalia area, then changed his mind? The discovery left Jim Hume scratching his head.[1]

Nearly four months passed quietly. Then suddenly, on July 27, 1888, just six months after Black Bart walked out of San Quentin, the Beiber-Redding stage was robbed by a solitary gunman. The Wells Fargo express box was smashed and the mail sacks slashed open. The bandit, who wore a cloth mask, escaped without a trace.

For a time there were no more stage robberies although the bandit who held up the Beiber-Redding stage had not been caught. Then, on November 8, the Downieville-Nevada City stage was robbed by a lone gunman on Ditch Hill, not far from Blue Tent. Again, the bandit escaped with the contents of the Wells Fargo express box and mail sacks. The express box had contained less than one hundred dollars in coin, but it had also held a $2,200 gold brick with the name H. Scammon stamped on it in several places.

Wells Fargo Detective Chief James Hume went to Nevada City to take on the investigation of this latest robbery. After in-

Ten months after his release from prison, Black Bart again became a stage robbery suspect, according to Well's Fargo's James Hume. On November 30, 1888 Wells Fargo issued this circular listing Bart as a suspect in July 27, November 8, and November 20, 1888 robberies, and included in it a detailed description of him. It is now believed Hume knew Black Bart was not involved, but issued the circular to make the real bandit less cautious.

WELLS, FARGO & CO'S EXPRESS.

SPECIAL OFFICER'S DEPARTMENT.

SAN FRANCISCO, November 30, 1888.

On the twenty-seventh day of July last, the stage from Bieber, Modoc Co., to Redding, Shasta Co., was robbed by one man of the U. S. mail and Wells, Fargo & Co's treasure box, the latter containing only $31.75. The amount obtained from the mail is not known but would probably be several hundred dollars.

On November 8th, the stage from Downieville to Nevada City was robbed near "Nigger Tent" by one man, who rifled three U. S. mail bags and Wells, Fargo & Co's treasure, getting from the latter $20.00 coin and a gold bar of the value of $2,500.00. Weight of bar, 127.77-100 ounces; fineness, 980; size, 9¼ inches in length by 2 9-16 inches wide and 1 inch thick, stamped on bottom, H. Scammon across the corners and in centre.

Wells, Fargo & Co. will give one-quarter the value of the bar for its recovery, or proportionately for any part thereof. It is not improbable that it may be cut and offered for sale or away in fragments.

On the twentieth of November, the stage from Eureka, Humboldt Co., to Ukiah, Mendocino Co., was robbed by one man who got from the Express $664.74 coin and currency, and probably $1,000.00 from the seven mail bags which he rifled.

We have reason to believe that the robberies above described were committed by the notorious C. E. Boles, alias C. E. Bolton, alias Black Bart the Po. 8.

Between July, 1851, and November 4, 1883, he robbed twenty-eight stages in this State alone. He was released from the State Prison at San Quentin, January 23, 1888; spent two weeks in this city, then went to Modesto, Maslen, Merced and Visalia, leaving the latter place February 28, under the name of M. Moore.

DESCRIPTION.

EDUCATION, liberal; NATIVITY, New York; AGE, about sixty years; OCCUPATION, mining; HEIGHT, five feet eight inches in stocking; COMPLEXION, light; COLOR OF EYES, blue; BEARD, MUSTACHE, nearly white; HEAVY IMPERIAL, nearly white; SIZE OF FOOT, No. 6; WEIGHT, 160 lbs.; SIZE OF HAT, 7¼; does not use tobacco in any form, nor intoxicating liquors or opium. High forehead, points running well up into hair; large ears, standing well out from head; eyes, light blue and deep set; nose rather prominent and broad at base; high cheek bones; heavy gray brows; chin square and rather small; head large and long; size ?¼; two upper front teeth missing on right side of mouth, two lower teeth missing in centre; small mole on left cheek bone; scar on top of forehead, ? the side; scar inside of left wrist; shield in India ink on right upper r... ma... on right upper arm; forearms quite hairy; heavy

AGENTS OF WELLS, FARGO & CO.:

Upon receiving a supply of these circulars you are requested to make such distribution of them, retaining one in your office for future reference, that residents in the country surrounding your station will be supplied.

A number of posters will follow these circulars and they, also, are to be distributed in a like manner, so that not only residents of your town but those dwelling in regions remote from town, will be made acquainted with and become familiar with the features and general description of this notorious stage robber.

Respectfully,

J. B. HUME,

Special Officer, Wells, Fargo & Co.

133

terviewing the driver and passengers and reviewing the overall picture, Hume returned to San Francisco fairly well assured that both holdups had been the work of Black Bart–at least, that is what he indicated to eager newsmen who awaited him.

By November 14, Hume had drafted and had printed a four-sheet circular which was quietly distributed to Wells Fargo agents throughout California, but was not publicly displayed. Briefly, it listed details of both robberies and it contained Black Bart's photograph, physical description and method of operation. The closing paragraph of the circular stated: "We have reason to believe that the robberies above described were committed by C. E. Boles, alias, Charles Bolton, alias Black Bart, the Po8."

Hume cautioned his readers that there was not sufficient evidence to call for issuance of an arrest warrant at this time, but that it was the desire of Wells Fargo to locate the suspected Black Bart and keep his movements under careful scrutiny. "Do Not Arrest. Make careful inquiries–get your local peace officers interested. Wire any information obtained, at once, to the undersigned." And, of course, the circular was signed by James B. Hume.

Much to Jim Hume's chagrin, the circulars–only a few actually were distributed to Wells Fargo agents–brought back not a smattering of information on the whereabouts of Black Bart. If he had committed the robberies, or if he was even in the state, Bart was certainly lying low.

Two weeks later a lone, masked highwayman robbed the Eureka-Ukiah stage of approximately seven hundred dollars in coin and rifled the contents of eleven mail sacks. Again, there were no positive clues found at the robbery scene. The description given by the stage driver could have fit Black Bart or just about anybody else except Santa Claus.

No one of Black Bart's description had been seen in the area of the robberies, but Hume, at least at that time, seemed satisfied that Bart was the culprit. Hume told a *Chronicle* reporter he recognized the earmarks of the Black Bart style, yet he did not say exactly what they were. Nor did he mention if there were or were not "T-shaped" slashes in the canvas mail sacks. Newspapers, of course, leaped onto the story, and Black Bart was again in the headlines. The stories, many of them farfetched, stirred up some

134

public interest but no real information. Reporters pressed Hume for interviews, and, probably with some distaste, he granted them. He never was too fond of newsmen.

Yes, he recognized the method used in these stage holdups. No, he had not come upon any definite clues, or at least that's what he told the prying bevy of reporters. Hume may have had other information such as footprints or some form of evidence left at the robbery scenes. If he did he said nothing about them. Again he made no mention of any "T-shaped" slashes in mail sacks, and for some reason, possibly short memories, the reporters did not ask about them. Hume was emphatic in his answer to numerous queries that no poetry had been left by the bandit.[2]

Then, following the Eureka-Ukiah stage robbery–lo and behold!–A Mendocino County newspaper reported that a poem had been found at the robbery scene by some curious onlooker, and forthwith published it as the latest works of the Po8.

"So here I've stood while wind and rain
Have set the trees a-sobbin'
And risked my life for that damned stage
That wasn't worth the robbin'."

Jim Hume immediately discounted the verse as a hoax, stating the handwriting did not match Black Bart's. Also, said he and numerous other students of Black Bart, the poetry itself was a bit too smooth and grammatical in comparison with the Po8's doggerel that had been found at his earlier robbery scenes. The papers, of course, had another field day with it, and if Hume had any reservations about Black Bart's involvement in the three northern California robberies, the news editors did not.[3]

Headlines that Bart had returned to his old ways now were common, both in bay papers and in the weekly publications of the mining and lumber towns. The San Francisco-published periodical *The Wasp* printed a cartoon depicting a sprightly, well groomed dude labeled Black Bart flirting with a somewhat distressed damsel named Wells Fargo, under the caption, "Will he woo her again?"

And, although Hume apparently allowed his suspicions concerning the July and November stage robberies in Shasta and Mendocino counties to center on his old pal, Black Bart, he said flatly that a series of robberies during that same period in Santa Barbara and San Luis Obispo counties had no connection with the Po8.

Eventually news of the Eureka-Ukiah stage robbery grew stale and public interest in Black Bart's escapades, including his latest alleged verse, began to wane. Then, wherever he was, guilty or not guilty of this latest spate of stage robberies, the first of a series of stories broke in the *San Francisco Examiner* that–if he saw them–must have set Black Bart chuckling to himself. On that last day of November, the *Examiner*, which had been among the first to link Bart with this latest series of robberies, reversed itself and declared Bart an innocent victim of Wells Fargo's vindictive detective chief, Jim Hume. The story printed November 30, 1888 was a short, unobtrusive one.

Purportedly by one of the *Examiner's* far-flung correspondents, a man named Martin, the article reported that Charles Bolton, better known as the notorious stage robber Black Bart, had been seen in (visited) the town of Lakeport. Bart had been identified, according to the *Examiner* story, by a local man named George Vann, who had seen him years before at the McCrearey ranch. Whether there was even a smidgen of truth in the story or whether it was a plant is not known. William Randolph Hearst's editorial staff in those days was not above fabricating happenings out of thin air.

Two days later, however, the *Examiner* took aim on the story with all its big guns, and the Wells Fargo detective chief was its main target. On December 2, in the Sunday *Examiner*, a four-column story was headlined: HUME IS CONTRADICTED. HOW A GREAT DETECTIVE MADE A REPUTATION

The story led off with the text of a telegram from special correspondent Martin, who informed the *Examiner's* managing editor he had located "the famed Black Bart." Bart, he said, had agreed reluctantly to an interview only if his whereabouts were concealed. The story also included the managing editor's answering telegram, which instructed Martin to "spare no expense. Transmit story by rail–wires may leak."

Martin's story, if there even was a correspondent named Martin, missed no opportunity to create drama. The writer related that he reached Bart's hideout only after traveling by train followed by a harrowing mountain trip on horseback during which he nearly drowned while crossing a rain-swollen stream. He was rescued, he said, by a man who gave him shelter and who later turned out to be Black Bart. Martin quoted Black Bart as saying he was living in the backwoods for the very fact he feared that the law would try to trump up new charges against him.

At first reluctant to talk, the man opened up, said Martin, after he showed him clippings from the *San Francisco Chronicle* which quoted Detective Hume as saying that Bart had returned to stage robbery. Martin said Black Bart flatly denied Hume's accusations, stating they were lies.

The *Examiner* correspondent went on to quote Bart that he had not committed a single illegal act since being released from prison and that Hume and Wells Fargo simply were using him as a scapegoat. They were angry at him, he said, because he had refused to admit the twenty-eight robberies they accused him of committing.

"I told them I had robbed only one stage and that was the only one I would admit to," Martin quoted Bart as saying. Martin continued the interview with a statement by Bart that Hume, Thacker and Morse had pressed him to write a book in which he would admit all of the robberies and praise the Wells Fargo men for their great detective work which resulted in his capture. When he refused to cooperate, Bart reportedly told Martin, the Wells Fargo representatives dropped all aspects of friendship toward him. The *Examiner*'s story also quoted Bart as accusing Hume and San Quentin Prison Captain Charles Aull of trying to defraud him of his diamond ring and jewelry.

Upon reading the *Chronicle* story in which Hume called Black Bart "a pusillanimous wretch" and accused him of abandoning his family, Martin said Bart was angry and affronted. The story went on to say that Bart defended himself, stating he had tried to make a living for his family by farming. He said he left to find a better means of livelihood only after a living from farming proved impossible. Bart, according to Martin, sent money home to his wife and added that since Mary Boles was an expert seamstress

*This now
famous cartoon
was printed in
The Wasp, a
San Francisco
periodical,
shortly after
Black Bart's
release from
prison in 1888.
Like many West
Coast
newspapers and
magazines, the
Wasp's
publishers
anticipated that
Bart soon would
return to stage
robbery and his
harassment
of Wells
Fargo & Co.*
(Photo courtesy of
Wells Fargo and
Calaveras County
archives.)

WILL HE WOO HER AGAIN?

and dressmaker, she was able to earn her own living. The story went on to say that Bart knew if he disappeared, his financially well-off father would take care of Mary and that when his father died, he left her a substantial amount of money. It was not until her brother-in-law swindled her out of those savings that she met with financial trouble, said the story.

Martin closed his story with Bart's supposed account of how he had been driven to crime, of how he had traveled the Montana-Idaho mining country, bad luck dogging him all the way. He lost a profitable gold mine, said Martin, due to cupidity and greed of a dishonest partner. With no worthwhile employment to be found, Bart decided to return to California and begin a new life, said the story. The only thing he kept to tie himself to his former life, according to Martin, was a Bible, a gift from his wife when he enlisted in the army. This would be the Bible found in his room years later, when he was arrested.

The year 1875, said the story, found Charles E. Boles (he had not yet adopted the alias Black Bart) seeking gainful employment in Northern California. He paused at a remote ranch and asked if he might have something to eat, but the rancher, according to the correspondent's story, instead of inviting him to dinner, handed Boles a dish of table scraps. As he stared at the plate with obvious distaste, the rancher asked him, "What's the matter, isn't it good enough for a bum like you?"

According to the story, the man who was later to become known as Black Bart set the food remnants of the porch in front of the dog and replied, "This is the first time I have ever asked for anything, and it will be the last. Hereafter, when I want anything, I shall demand and take it."

Overall, the story was more of a condemnation of Wells Fargo and James Hume than an exoneration of Black Bart. But for the *Examiner* it had exactly the desired effect. It boosted readership and made Jim Hume mad as hell. In a letter to the *Examiner* a livid Hume called the story "a thorough falsehood, made up of distorted and villainous lies." He termed the man who wrote them "low, malignant and contemptible. The purported interview," he said, "is entirely the boldest of inventions–invented to vilify me, by a sneak too cowardly to sign his name." Hume apparently believed "Martin" to be an alias used by some *Examiner* editor who had never been within rifle range of Black Bart.

What seemed to most outrage the detective chief was the accusation that Black Bart had confessed only to the single, November 3, 1883, Funk Hill robbery and that his confessions to twenty-seven others was a falsehood cooked up by Hume and Wells Fargo to clear up unsolved crimes. Hume described the allegations as "another of the *Examiner*'s ingenious lies." He went on to say that following Bart's confession and sentencing in San Andreas for the Funk Hill robbery, he interviewed Bart in the presence of Calaveras County Sheriff Ben Thorn.

Hume said that in front of Ben Thorn, who, he said, "is an honest man," he had asked Bart, for the sake of clearing up company records, to list the robberies he had committed. Hume added that at the time, he believed Boles to be responsible only for twenty-one stage holdups. He said that following assurances that such a confession would not be used against him, the "Po8" confessed to a total of twenty-eight robberies committed between July 26, 1875 and November 3, 1883.

"That was exactly how the confessions came about," said the irate Hume, "and as witnesses I have Sheriff Thorn and another man, both of whom will swear honestly to what took place."

As for Bart's purported claim in the Martin interview that Hume had proposed he write a book about his stage robbery career which would have credited Hume with being a master sleuth, the detective chief called it an outright lie. He had never, he said, discussed a book of any kind with Charles E. Boles. Hume also angrily refuted the claim in Martin's story that he, Morse or Captain Aull had tried to wangle Bart's diamonds and jewelry from him.

Hume said he believed the diamond ring which Bart wore was the one that had been taken from the Wells Fargo express box in Bart's 1878 robbery of the Quincy-Oroville stage. He said his only reference to the ring was to tell Black Bart that if it was the stolen ring, it should be returned to the Plumas County businessman who owned it. Hume said that when Bart denied it was the ring taken in the LaPorte stage robbery, he dropped the subject and it was not brought up again.

The *Examiner*, of course, was delighted in Hume's angry response. The paper's managing editor sent a reporter around to interview him and he was not disappointed. Again, Hume said the so-called Martin interview with Black Bart was "a falsehood made up of distorted and villainous lies and the man who wrote them was a low, contemptible cur."

"Before you go," Hume told the Examiner's scribe, "I want to say that the scoundrel who directed this attack on me is a vile miscreant—and I say it again—a cowardly contemptible cur. I live at 1466 Eighth Street in Oakland. My office is Room 28, over the Wells Fargo and Company's, and I'm always in!"

It was the beginning of a war of words. The *Examiner* reporter's interview with Hume was printed the following day under the headline, "Mr. Hume Gets Angry." In addition to the actual interview with Hume, the *Examiner* added a bit more lineage, including an editorial that took a few more pot shots at him. The editorial, titled "Keep Cool Mr. Hume," consisted of the following: "Mr. Hume, the great detective of Wells Fargo & Company, seems to be very angry with the *Examiner* because the *Examiner* has given Black Bart's version of some matters in which both were interested. Mr. Hume loses his temper, applies bad names to the correspondent who wrote what Black Bart said and accuses the reporter of malignant designs upon his (Mr. Hume's) well earned reputation. Mr. Hume's criticism of the reporter for not signing his name is childish. It is not the custom in news offices to allow signatures to news matter.

"The great detective should remember he had his say about Black Bart and said some very hard things about the famous robber. It is only fair to let Boles have his say. And more over, Mr. Hume should remember that the *Examiner* exists to give the news, hires men to collect it and gives more interesting news than any other newspaper.

"It does not follow that the *Examiner* endorses Black Bart or its correspondent is responsible for any misstatements made by that interesting and much missed person. Mr. Hume should cool down."

One thing Jim Hume apparently failed to remember is the old political axiom that advises against getting into arguments "with people who buy ink by the barrel." When the *Chronicle* sent a man out to interview Hume he had not cooled down. He again called the *Examiner's* interview with Black Bart "a pack of lies."

When asked by the *Chronicle* reporter what in the *Examiner's* story he objected to, Hume replied: "All of it." Hume said the man, Martin, if there was such a man, never saw or talked to Charles Boles and that virtually everything in his story was inaccurate and probably had been deliberately distorted. He added that it was written simply to damage his reputation and the reputation of Wells Fargo.

"Why would the *Examiner* print such an article?" asked the *Chronicle* man.

"I cannot tell you," replied Hume, "unless it is animosity toward a man who has never known or injured the author. It is a dime-novel story that will delude no one. Why Black Bart himself, as accomplished a scoundrel as he is, wouldn't have stooped to anything so low."

If Hearst or the *Examiner*'s managing editor, still miffed at Wells Fargo and Hume for allowing opposition newspapers to scoop the *Examiner* concerning Black Bart's 1883 arrest, had planted the story simply to irritate Hume, they certainly had succeeded.

Then, once again in a letter printed in the *Chronicle* on December 5, 1888, Mary Boles entered the picture, defending her husband's innocence. Apparently she was keeping close track of the situation concerning her husband's disappearance and on the debate over whether he had returned to his stage robbery career. The fact that he had refused to return to her seemed not at all to have swayed her faith in him.

"My family and I believe today that Hume and Company now are after an innocent man," said Mrs. Boles. She accused Hume of holding an old grudge and that his belief that Bart had returned to robbery was based on his dislike for her husband rather than on fact. Her long and somewhat rambling letter pointed to her husband's believed rehabilitation and observed that while in prison he had become a trusted helper and associate of Dr. Rich in the San Quentin hospital.

"He told us over and over again," she said, "that while God gave him breath he would never again lift his hand to a dishonorable act that would disgrace us further." She also again raised Bart's allegation that Hume was seeking revenge for his refusal while in prison, to write a book lauding Hume's merits as a detective and protector of Wells Fargo. She closed her letter with still another assertion that her husband had assured her he would never return to crime. She stated emphatically that, although he had been unable to return to Missouri, she still believed in him.

Just where Black Bart may have been while all this verbal sparring was taking place is to this day unknown. Reported sightings of him had ended–even those so commonly received by every law enforcement and investigative agency, which obviously were the work of crackpots and cranks. It was just as if Black Bart had somehow dropped through a crack in the earth.

The following day, December 6, ignoring Mary Boles' protests of her husband's innocence, the *Chronicle* heaped more fuel on the growing newspaper feud. It quoted Jim Hume as saying he now was sure the latest Mendocino County robbery was the work of Black Bart. "It bore his unmistakable trademarks."[4]

The *San Francisco Examiner* countered with a blast which stated: "IT IS NOT BLACK BART."

Hearst's writers listed sundry reasons why the robberies were not the work of the famous bandit, and for the first time raised the now famous allegation that Wells Fargo & Company had pensioned off Black Bart to keep him from returning to the road. Jim Hume, angered again, publicly derided the story as "pure hogwash."

How long this battle of words over Black Bart's possible re-entry into the field of crime might have gone on is a matter of conjecture. Possibly it would have continued until every *Examiner* and *Chronicle* reader, sick of the dispute, canceled their subscription in disgust, or until Jim Hume shot William Randolph Hearst –or, more likely, died of apoplexy. As it turned out, it was San Quentin Prison's newly appointed warden, John J. McComb, who saved the day and probably Hume's sanity.

McComb accidentally let slip to a *Chronicle* reporter the fact that Hume had recently paid a visit to the prison. He had come there, said McComb, to check the physical description and dental records of recently released convict and former stage robber J. A. Wright, whom he believed was responsible for the latest rash of stage holdups.

Wright, alias John Garvin, had committed five stage robberies between December 28, 1876 and February 24, 1877. They included the Angels Camp-Milton, San Juan-Marysville, Murphys-Milton, Jackson-Ione and Sonora-Milton stages. He always worked alone, using a revolver instead of a shotgun as a weapon of intimidation. He had been convicted in Calaveras County and in May, 1877, sentenced to fifteen years in prison. After serving nine years, he was released in 1886. However, his earlier attempts at pardon or parole had been denied and reportedly, he blamed Wells Fargo for blocking them. Supposedly at the time of the denial of his early release he had said of James Hume and Wells Fargo officials in general, "I'll make those sons-of-bitches pay for that yet."

143

Arrival of the stage from Stockton at its Metropolitan Hotel was the highlight of the day in San Andreas. Usually a full load of passengers accompanied the mail and Wells Fargo express box.

The *Chronicle* story blew the Black Bart's return to robbery theory out of the water. Questioned pointedly, Hume admitted it was Wright and not Black Bart who now had become his latest prime suspect. He also divulged that these latest robberies had been committed by a man armed with a revolver rather than a shotgun. Bart, in all his twenty-eight robberies, had used only a shotgun, which he maintained was never loaded. Also, the Wells Fargo detective chief reluctantly admitted, the recent robberies were the work of a man somewhat taller than Black Bart, who traveled on horseback. Black Bart, in all of his eight years of stage robbery, had never once used a horse.

The newspapers immediately jumped on the supposition that Hume had been using Bart simply as a stalking horse for the purpose of possibly lulling Wright into carelessness or complacency. The *Examiner*, of course, made the most of it.

XX

If J. A. Wright, alias John Garvin, really was the stage robber Wells Fargo was looking for, the question still remains, where was Black Bart? Why had he so mysteriously dropped from sight? Also, reporters wanted to know, when had Wells Fargo's James Hume dropped him from its list of robbery suspects? Not all of Hume's statements to various newsmen concerning Bart's status as a suspect, or where he might be, seemed to be in accord.

At one point during a December interview with a *Chronicle* reporter, Hume said he had heard of Black Bart as late as November 23, 1888, shortly following the Eureka-Ukiah stage robbery. Since that time, Hume said, he understood that Bart had left the state.

Not long after that he told an *Examiner* newsman, who cornered him for an interview, that he did not feel Bart was responsible for the most recent robberies and the last time he had heard of him was on April 6. At that time, he said, Bart was leaving California for the far East. But, Jim Hume could be devious, and there were those, including Sheriff Ben Thorn and San Joaquin County's Sheriff Tom Cunningham, who whispered to associates that Hume still suspected Charles Boles, alias Black Bart. They believed he had deliberately manufactured the J. A. Wright story to lull Bart into complacency.

At any rate, the Hearst paper refused to accept Hume's story of the April sighting of Black Bart or rumors he had left for Japan or China. The newspaper just as adamantly pooh-poohed the theory that Hume was using the Wright story to lure Bart out of hiding so he could be arrested.

Black Bart was not robbing stages, said the *Examiner,* and Wells Fargo and its detective chief very well knew he was not. Bart had not returned to stage robbery, said the paper, because Wells Fargo had placed him on its payroll. The banking and express company was paying Charles Bolton $125 per month to leave its express boxes alone and had been doing so since shortly after he had been released from prison.

The *Examiner* quoted Bart as saying, "I'm a detective now, myself, and I've just received another month's salary."

The story went on to say the express company had wanted to pay Bart his wages on a daily basis, presumably so that its agents could keep their eyes on him. It said he insisted, however, on being paid by the month so he could travel freely and pick up his salary at any Wells Fargo office. The writer of the story closed with the statement that Bart had resumed gold mining and, with a partner, was working a small placer claim at an undisclosed location.[1]

It was a typical *Examiner* story of that period, filled with statements and quotes that could not be substantiated. Yet, it brought into the open a question that to this day remains one of the intriguing mysteries of those golden days of San Francisco, Wells Fargo and the Mother Lode and adds to the many myths that surround the Black Bart saga. Did Wells Fargo & Company indeed, with or without the blessings of its chief of detectives, James Hume, pay the man known as Black Bart to leave its express shipments alone?

From the moment the *Examiner*'s story hit the street, the company was busy denying it. "Not a word of truth to it," exploded James Hume, and to emphasize his and the express company's denial of any pension for the famed bandit, Wells Fargo ran a paid ad in the *San Francisco Chronicle,* stating: CHARLES E. BOLTON IS NOT AND NEVER HAS BEEN ON WELLS FARGO'S PAYROLL.

146

Hume also, again and again, made public denials that Bart was being paid by Wells Fargo. However, the story persists to this day. But the pundits are divided. There are western history buffs and persons of note who say the payoffs were made, yet, just as many other students of Black Bart and Wells Fargo lore deny that it could have happened. Western historian and author James Henry Jackson was among those who said there was not a shred of truth to it.[2] Lucius Beebee and Charles Clegg commented in their *U.S. West, the Saga of Wells Fargo* "that historians of the banking and express company will look in vain for any record of precise conduct of the company's internal affairs during the last several decades of the nineteenth century." They said it was a very closed corporation and what its right hand, representing Wells Fargo Banking did, was generally unknown, except among the highest echelon of executives and directors of its left hand, representing Wells Fargo Express. If there ever was any official record of such a transaction, it is gone, for a great many of Wells Fargo's records were destroyed in the San Francisco earthquake and fire of 1906.

Among those who expressed belief that Black Bart was pensioned off was Evelyn Wells Podesta. While she agreed that Wells Fargo records show no such arrangement, she also pointed out that there was considerable of Wells Fargo's affairs during those years that were never entered on their ledgers. Calaveras County Superior Judge J. A. Smith, member of a pioneer family, whose law practice and judgeship spanned forty-nine years, beginning in 1909, chose to believe that Bart was paid off by the express company. Questioned during his retirement years concerning his knowledge of the Black Bart era, Judge Smith agreed with Mrs. Podesta. "Of course they paid him," he said. "It was common knowledge."

The flurry of excitement concerning the alleged Black Bart payoff died down and gradually interest in where he might have gone also waned. The American public, even a century ago, did not possess a very lengthy attention span. Those who did remember Black Bart, including various lawmen, believed he either had left California or was dead.

But rumors kept cropping up. He was reported to have been seen in China. It was said he had gone to Australia, and that he was living in Japan. There were other reports that Bart had gone

147

to Nevada, and there were claims he was living in Oklahoma's Indian Territory. The sheriff at Cripple Creek, Colorado, wired Wells Fargo he was holding a man identified as Black Bart, only to be notified by Hume that the former stage robber, whether using the name Boles, Bolton or some other alias, was not wanted in the golden state.

At one point Hume sent Jonathan Thacker to Olanthe, Kansas, where a man arrested for the theft of $400 claimed to be Black Bart. Thacker immediately identified the suspect as H. L. Gorton, a former California train robber who served seven years in Folsom Prison and had since sunk to petty thievery. Wrote Thacker in his report, "Wells Fargo is not interested in cheapskate burglars and chicken thieves." However, at the close of his report he did touch on the subject of Black Bart, stating that following his release from San Quentin, Bart went to Utah, then to Montana and on to Idaho. From there, said Thacker, in Seattle, Washington, he boarded the steamer *Empress of China*, bound for Japan. In closing his report, Thacker said, "He is in that country now, and at any rate, he is straight as a string."[3]

By 1892, Mary Boles, still in Hannibal, Missouri, listed herself in the city directory as the widow of Charles E. Boles. It is possible, of course, that she knew more than she was telling, but also, the listing of herself as a widow may have been done simply as a matter of convenience. Apparently, if nothing else, Mrs. Boles now had lost hope that her husband ever would return to her. She apparently still was living with a married daughter, with sewing and dressmaking providing her only income. If Mrs. Boles' assertion that her husband was dead was just a guess, her guess was at least as good as anyone's.

If Thacker's statement was true, that Bart, after his release from prison, had moved through several states, then left for the Orient, again a primary question arises. From where did the money come to finance his travels? Did he have money hidden away when he was sentenced to prison? Wells Fargo's Jim Hume estimated that the loot which Bart removed from the company's express boxes in twenty-eight robberies over an eight-year period totaled something less than twelve thousand dollars. However, that did not include what he may have found in the sacks of mail that virtually every stagecoach carried. Hume often quoted Bart as saying that his take from the mail pouches usually exceeded that which he found in the Wells Fargo express boxes. There was no way of ever ascertaining just how much Bart may have gotten from the mails. But, if Bart did have a secret cache of funds created at the expense of Wells Fargo, he would not have been the last San Francisco inhabitant to have done so.

* * *

The man San Francisco came to know as Baron Karl Hartmann and Black Bart had little in common except a taste for the better things in life. Both were essentially believers in nonviolence and both were free with Wells Fargo funds. And, both were part of that gilded era of the city by the bay.

Baron Hartmann arrived in San Francisco during the early years of the 1890's. Identifying himself as the brother of the late Baroness Hartmann of Westphalia, he took up residence in the Golden West Hotel, but soon moved into the glittering quarters of William Ralston's Palace Hotel. E.S. "Lucky" Baldwin's Market Street Hotel and the posh Palace bar soon were among his favorite watering spots, and he drank only the best of imported spirits. There and in other fashionable locations, the baron rubbed elbows and often exchanged views with San Francisco's own nabobs and robber barons.

Middle aged, portly and aristocratic in appearance, with graying, well-groomed hair, Baron Hartmann was undeniably flush with cash. He spoke fluent German and also conversed well in French, Italian and Danish. If the baron stood out from those native representatives of San Francisco's wealthy set, it was because of his somewhat flamboyant dress. Eschewing the conservative suits with clawhammer coat styles, the baron outfitted himself in obviously expensive but colorful suits that tended to run to large plaids. He was a frequent visitor to the race track, where he often wagered sizable sums. Few were those, down on their luck from an afternoon of choosing the wrong horse, who could not look to the baron for a substantial loan.

When the owner of an Oregon Street saloon—another of the baron's favorite haunts—found himself in financial trouble, Baron Hartmann graciously loaned him $6,000 at low interest. He made other loans, mostly to drinking spots, and one investment involved financing the owner of a secret bitters formula and outfitting him with a delivery wagon with electric lights. The venture failed when the bitters magnate, possibly after imbibing too heaving of his own 80 percent alcohol product, drove his wagon in front of a fast moving freight train.

Baron Hartmann headed for New York, but after arriving became lonesome and sent for his girl friend of the moment, a young sporting lady who, when not following her trade, spent her leisure hours at the race track. He sent her $1,000 and told her to join him in Manhattan, but instead, she used the money to set herself and a friend up as bookmakers at the race track. Angry, the love-smitten baron returned to San Francisco, and that became his greatest mistake.

Baron Hartmann had hardly stepped from the train in San Francisco when he was greeted by a gentleman who introduced himself as James Hume of Wells Fargo. Hume suggested they visit his headquarters for a quiet business discussion. It turned out that the Baron Karl Hartmann was none other than Dutch Charlie, known by every hobo from the Pacific coast to Indiana. His affluence, rather than originating in Westphalia, had come from the robbery of a Southern Pacific Company express car two years earlier, on the outskirts of Sacramento, probably about where the city of West Sacramento now stands.

Dutch Charlie had taken no part in the holdup. Instead, he and his partner, August Kohler, had watched the proceedings from the safety of their hobo camp as train robber Jack Brady and his gang took $50,000 of Wells Fargo money from the express car. There had been some shooting. With one of their gang wounded, Brady and his cohorts buried the money at the robbery scene and fled. As soon as the train robbers were out of sight, Dutch Charlie and Kohler dug up the loot, of which Charlie appropriated all but enough to allow Kohler a week-long binge in nearby Sacramento.

Charlie left for San Francisco and when Kohler finally located him nearly two years later, strutting down Market Street in his finery, Charlie refused even to recognize him. The angry and affronted Kohler made a hasty trip to the office of Wells Fargo and shortly thereafter, the Baron Karl Hartmann's fortunes changed.

150

But, the Wells Fargo agents found little to bring them pleasure in the baron's plush suite. There were numerous fashionable hats and pairs of patent leather shoes, a gaudy array of ratcatcher suits, along with notes on the defunct bitters company and a couple of failing saloons. Disappointingly, there was damned little remaining hard cash.

Said Dutch Charlie when they sentenced him to three years in Folsom Prison, "My only regret is that I didn't have time to spend all of Wells Fargo's money before they caught me."

Again, wherever he was, Black Bart must have chuckled to himself when he heard about Dutch Charlie's two-year spree at Wells Fargo's expense. Although it is doubtful they ever met, together Bart and Charlie constituted a colossal pain to Wells Fargo and its special agents. Intriguingly, they pulled off their capers without physically injuring a single person or firing a single shot.

Actually, by 1900 and the Baron's heyday, Wells Fargo had pretty well written off Black Bart as a potential criminal or possible stage robbery suspect. He had not been heard of for a long time, although now and then some unsubstantiated rumor that he had been seen in Idaho or Panama or some remote Texas town circulated until it died a natural death. Still, when some lone gunman in California or Nevada occasionally relieved a stage of its express box shipment, the name of Black Bart inevitably cropped up on local newspaper pages. But, by the turn of the century stage robberies had drastically decreased, and Wells Fargo and Jim Hume were far more preoccupied with train robberies during the last decade of the nineteenth century.

Furthermore, by 1900 Bart would have been nearly seventy years old, hardly a desirable age at which to re-enter the stage robbery business. Also, his nemesis, James Hume, who of all law enforcement officers remembered him best–if not fondly–was busy and he also was getting no younger. Concerned with train robberies and in failing health, Hume was by then largely directing his company's field operations from the relative comfort of his office. He would have had little time to think about Black Bart.

Nevertheless, there were times when the memory of Charles Boles must have crossed Hume's mind. Certainly, no man with Hume's natural curiosity could help but wonder from time to time what really happened to the bandit who had led him such a frustrating chase for eight years.

How much James Hume really knew of Bart's whereabouts or movements after he went underground in February or March of 1888, no one probably will ever know. No doubt, Hume and his agents did keep track of Bart for a while, at least until he disappeared in Visalia. If indeed it was he who registered in the Visalia hotel as a Mr. Moore and left a valise there.... But, how much Hume really knew about Bart's movements after that, and how much of his purported knowledge was bluff remains unknown. Certainly, Hume believed not a word of the *Examiner*'s stories concerning Bart's activities after he got out of prison. Until his dying day, Hume angrily refuted the accusation that Wells Fargo pensioned off the old stage robber. Also, it is highly unlikely, even though Hume repeated such reports, that he really believed Black Bart had taken off for Japan, China, Australia or some other foreign land.

It would seem more plausible that Bart, if he left California, would have gone to Idaho, Montana or some other western state. There seemed, during the early and mid-nineties, to be many versions of where Bart might have gone. One story that circulated after the turn of the century was that during those years he was living in Oakland and working in the Ferry Building on San Francisco's Embarcadero, right under the noses of prying newsmen, where Wells Fargo could keep an eye on him.

Quite possibly, the last time Bart was mentioned as a holdup suspect was in Placer County, following a July 3, 1903, robbery of an Auburn-Foresthill stage. On that occasion a lone bandit with a shotgun made off with an undetermined amount of money after shooting a lead stage horse named Old Joe.

"Damn you," shouted stage driver Henry Wise. "You've killed the best lead horse in the county."

The bandit was never caught, but even though there was talk that Black Bart had returned, few took the suggestion very seriously. By that time Bart would have been seventy-five years old. Old Joe was buried at the robbery site, and for years Henry Wise returned each July 3 to place a small American flag on his grave.

Other farfetched stories of Black Bart periodically kept cropping up. Nothing seemed too ludicrous to print, particularly in

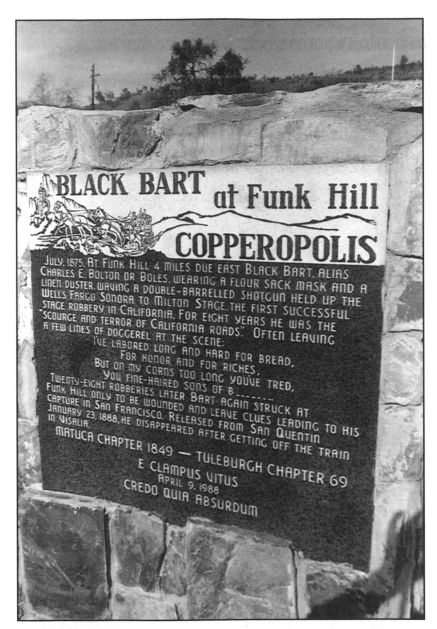

The Black Bart plaque in the old copper mining town of Copperopolis tells the story. However, Bart's first Funk Hill robbery was far from being California's first successful stage holdup.

the Eastern press. The *New York Daily Times* came out with a story of Bart turning train robber and successfully accomplishing the robbery by dressing several fence posts in scarecrow fashion to simulate members of a bandit gang. As late as 1946 a *New York World Telegram* reporter in search of a Sunday feature printed a Black Bart story which stated his first robbery had been committed with a walking stick. Said the writer, Bart playfully pointed the stick at a passing stage driver who became so frightened he threw down the express box. Thus, finding stage robbery so easy, said the New York journalist, Bart quit his Sierra County teaching position to become a highwayman. If Jim Hume had been alive he probably would have become sick to his stomach.

It does seem strange that a man whose reputation and face was as widely known, at least in law enforcement circles, as Black Bart's could simply disappear and never be seen again. One theory is that he returned to some part of the East where he was not known and established a new life. It is possible, of course, that he could have done that and supported a new wife and possibly a family, on wages earned as a drug clerk. He also could have turned to mining in Idaho, Colorado or some other western mining center, although it does not appear Bart was that enamored with physical labor.

Then, there is always that sighting of a man identified in 1909 as Black Bart by the owner of the Murphys Hotel. Certainly Rose Schwoerer, who as a girl worked at the hotel, believed it to be true. Reportedly, in 1917, a New York newspaper printed a brief obituary of a Charles E. Boles, a Civil War veteran. If this was the Charles Boles of Black Bart fame he would have been eighty-seven years old when he went to the great beyond.

Yet, with the promise of solving the Black Bart mystery for all time, an intriguing story comes whispering out of Nevada's Comstock Lode country.

Just after daybreak one warm day in the summer of 1888, a masked bandit, shotgun poised, stepped into the path of a six-horse stage as it headed down Geiger Grade on the Virginia City-Reno run. Whether the gunman had time to instruct the driver to throw down the box is academic. The driver did not drop the express box, nor did the messenger beside him drop his shotgun.

Instead, twin loads of buckshot from the messenger's double barreled, 10 gauge L. C. Smith took the stage robber before his finger pulled the triggers of his own gun. The bandit was dead before he hit the ground.

They didn't stand on ceremony in the Virginia City area
during the 1880's. The stage, hardly pausing at the shooting scene,
continued the thirty mile trip to Reno. From that city the Wells
Fargo agent telegraphed Storey County sheriff John S. McCullough
in Virginia City to inform him of the attempted robbery and the
bandit's death.

The sheriff, the coroner, several men who would serve as a
coroner's jury, and a few hangers-on rode to the robbery scene,
where a coroner's inquest was held on the spot. The body of the
deceased gunman carried no identification, and the shooting was
ruled as amply justified.

It was decided there was little need or justification for trans-
porting to Virginia City the body of an unidentified stage robber,
which was ripening fast in the summer sun. Shovels carried to the
scene for just such a purpose were put to use. The deceased highwayman, wrapped in a couple of saddle blankets, was buried in a
shallow grave beside the road, among the sagebrush and juni-
pers, only yards from where he had died.

The attempted robbery and death of the bandit of course
caused some stir and commentary in Virginia City and Reno papers, along with a bit of local speculation as to who the culprit
might have been. The local Wells Fargo agent filed the required
report on the attempted robbery and the subsequent shooting,
and no doubt eventually the messenger and stage driver received
company rewards. But, the public soon lost interest and the incident was generally forgotten.

Of course, there was talk among those who had gone to the
death scene and participated in the inquest and burial, including
the sheriff. Several of those men, former Californians who may
have seen a photograph or sketch of Black Bart, remarked on the
possible resemblance of the buckshot-riddled body to the famed
California bandit. But there was no absolute proof. None of the
men who spoke of Black Bart had ever seen the noted stage robber in person, and anyway, he was no longer a wanted man.[4]

If the Storey County sheriff gave the talk of Black Bart any credence, it apparently was not enough for him to bother contacting California authorities or Wells Fargo's detective chief, James Hume. Had he done so, there is little doubt that Hume or Jonathan Thacker, if only to satisfy their own curiosity, would have come to Virginia City and the burial site. Wells Fargo in the past, as in the case of Mike Tovey's killing of W. C. Jones at Aurora in 1880, had not been squeamish about exhuming the body of a dead bandit in order to make a positive identification. And, of course, a positive identification would have taken Bart off the list of possible suspects in subsequent robberies.

Whether the shotgun-toting bandit was the notorious Black Bart or some other luckless stage robber remains a matter of conjecture. Today, even the site of the grave itself is lost.

One point appears certain. Black Bart dropped from sight in 1888. Other than vague reports or perhaps self-serving hearsay, there is no really substantiated evidence he was ever seen again.

Did he, as many believe, return to the East, or did he lose himself in some small Western or Midwestern town, leading a sedentary life as a model citizen? Or, as seems most likely, did he return to a life of banditry and now lie in some forgotten, sandy Nevada grave?

BLACK BART
STAGE ROBBERIES

July 26, 1875 – November 3, 1883

No. 1. July 26, 1875. Calaveras County at Funk Hill on Sonora-Milton Road, four miles east of Copperopolis. One hundred sixty dollars in gold notes taken from Wells Fargo express box, plus other undetermined cash and contents of U.S. Mail pouch. John Shine, driver.

No. 2. December 28, 1875. Yuba County on North San Juan-Marysville Road, four miles north of Smartsville. Small, undisclosed amount taken from Wells Fargo box and mail sacks. Mike Hogan, driver.

No. 3. June 2, 1876. Siskiyou County on Roseburg, Oregon-Yreka, California Route. A nighttime robbery two miles south of Oregon border and five miles north of Cottonwood. Estimated eighty dollars taken from Wells Fargo box and unknown amount from mail sacks. A. C. Adams, driver.

No. 4. August 3, 1877. Sonoma County between Fort Ross and Duncan Mills, on the Russian River, four miles southeast of Fort Ross. Taken from Wells Fargo box, $300 in gold coin and a check for $305. Unknown amount from mail pouches. Here, scribbled on a way bill taken from the Wells Fargo box, Black Bart left the first of his bits of famous doggerel verse:

> *"I've labored long and hard for bread*
> *For honor and for riches*
> *But on my corns too long you've tread*
> *You fine haired sons of bitches.*
> *Black Bart, the P o 8."*

No. 5. July 25, 1878. Butte County on the Oroville-Quincy Road one mile from Berry Creek sawmill. Taken from the Wells Fargo box, $379 in coin, a two hundred-dollar diamond ring and a twenty-five-dollar silver watch. An undetermined amount of money was taken from the mail sacks. Also, found in the smashed Wells Fargo box the next day was another of Bart's bits of poetry:

"Here I lay me down to sleep
To wait the coming morrow
Perhaps success perhaps defeat
And everlasting sorrow.
Let come what will, I'll try it on
My condition can't be worse,
But if there's money in the box,
It's munny in my purse.
Black Bart, the P o 8."

No. 6. July 30, 1878. Plumas County, on the LaPorte to Oroville Road, five miles south of LaPorte. From Wells Fargo express box was taken fifty dollars in gold nuggets and a silver watch. The bandit also slit open the mail sacks, from which an undetermined amount was taken. D. E. Barry, driver.

No. 7. October 2, 1878. Mendocino County on Cahto to Ukiah route, twelve miles from Ukiah at spot on Forsyth Creek which is known as Robber's Rock. A total of forty dollars and another watch taken from Wells Fargo box. Mail sacks were slit open with undetermined loss. Alec Fowler, driver.

No. 8. October 3, 1878. Mendocino county on the Covelo-Ukiah Road, ten miles from Potter Valley near the intersection of the Potter-Redwood Valley Road. An undisclosed amount taken from the Wells Fargo box, and mail sacks were slashed open. Bandit was tracked considerable distance toward Colusa County before trail was lost. Nate Waltrip, driver.

No. 9. June 21, 1879. Butte County on the Forbestown-Oroville Road, three miles west of Forbestown. Wells Fargo reportedly suffered only a small loss from its express box. An unknown amount was taken from the mail. Dave Quadlin, driver.

No. 10. October 25, 1879. Shasta County on the Roseburg, Oregon-Yreka-Redding run, between Bass Station and Buckeye. This was a night robbery. Only a small amount was reported lost in the robbery of the Wells Fargo box, but an estimated fourteen hundred dollars was taken in cash from the mail pouches. Jim Smithson, driver.

No. 11. October 27, 1879. Shasta County, Alturas-Redding stage road, twelve miles northeast of Millville near the Canyon House. An undetermined amount of money taken from express box and mail pouches. Bandit fled west toward Sacramento River and town of Red Bluff, fifty miles away. Ed Payne, driver.

No. 12. July 22, 1880. Sonoma County, on Point Arena-Duncan Mills Road, three miles southeast of Henry's Hotel. The amount taken from the Wells Fargo express box and mail sacks was undetermined. Martin McClennan, driver. There has always been controversy as to whether the man who committed this robbery was Black Bart.

No. 13. September 1, 1880. Shasta County, on Weaverville-Redding Road near Last Chance Station, on Trinity Mountain. The bandit ordered stage driver Charley Creamer to throw down the express box and mail sacks, then unsuccessfully attempted to open an iron box attached to the stage while he held Creamer at gun point beside his team. Wells Fargo's loss amounted to little more than one hundred dollars. Contents of the mail pouches unknown.

No. 14. September 16, 1880. Jackson County, Oregon, on the Roseburg, Oregon-Yreka, California Road, one mile north of the Oregon-California line. This was another nighttime robbery which netted Black Bart approximately a thousand dollars from the Wells Fargo express box, plus an undetermined amount from the U.S. Mail.

No. 15. September 23, 1880. Jackson County, Oregon, on the Roseburg, Oregon-Redding Road about three miles north of the state line. The gunman ordered the stage driver to stand beside his team while the bandit smashed open the Wells Fargo box, which was bolted to the stage. He obtained a thousand dollars in gold dust and the contents of the mail sacks. (There is controversy whether Nort Eddings or George Chase was the driver.)

No. 16. November 20, 1880. Siskiyou County, on the Roseburg, Oregon-Redding, California route, a mile south of the Oregon-California border. The stage was stopped shortly after dark by a masked gunman who fled with a single mail sack after stage driver Joe Mason swung at him with a hatchet as the bandit attempted to help the driver lift the heavy express box out of the stage. Wells Fargo suffered no loss. Contents of the mail sack were unknown.

No. 17. August 31, 1881. Siskiyou County, on Roseburg, Oregon-Yreka Road, ten miles north of Yreka. Stage was stopped at 1:00 a.m. by a man standing beside a roadside campfire. Driver John Sullaway was ordered to throw down the express box and mail pouches. Amount of Wells Fargo's loss was not divulged.

No. 18. October 8, 1881. Shasta County. A midnight robbery on the Yreka-Redding Road at Bass Hill, fourteen miles north of Redding. The bandit took advantage of bright moonlight to halt stage and force driver Horace Williams off the stage while he smashed the Wells Fargo box. Wells Fargo's loss, sixty dollars.

No. 19. October 11, 1881. Shasta County, Alturas to Redding stage driven by Lewis Brewster, robbed at Montgomery Creek as driver was stopped for a harness repair. Wells Fargo's loss remained undisclosed.

No. 20. December 15, 1881. Yuba County. Stage from Camptonville robbed four miles east of Dobbins on the Downieville-Marysville Road. Driver George Sharpe forced to throw down the Wells Fargo express box and the mail. Wells Fargo agent said his company suffered only a small loss.

No. 21. December 27, 1881. Nevada County, on the North San Juan-Marysville Road. The stage was robbed at Bridgeport where a covered wooden bridge spanned the South Fork of the Yuba River, north of Smartsville. Wells Fargo reported express box and mail sacks taken, but small loss. Stage driver not identified.

No. 22. January 26, 1882. Mendocino County. The Ukiah-Cloverdale stage robbed six miles north of Cloverdale. Wells Fargo express boxes and mail pouches taken, but losses to the express company and to mail customers were unknown. Harry Forse, driver.

No. 23. June 14, 1882. Mendocino County near Robber's Rock, two miles from Little Lake on the Willits-Ukiah Road. Stage driver Thomas B. Forse was robbed of the Wells Fargo express box and the mail. Black Bart escaped with an estimated three hundred dollars from the box and an unknown amount from the mail.

No. 24. July 13, 1882. Plumas County, five miles west of LaPorte on the LaPorte-Oroville run. Wells Fargo messenger

George Hackett fired at a flour sack-masked man who leaped into the road in front of the stage. His intended target escaped, leaving a bullet-perforated hat in the road, and Black Bart wore a faint scar from that bullet on his temple for the remainder of his life.

No. 25. September 17, 1882. Shasta County on the Yreka-Redding Road at Bass Hill. Black Bart stopped stage driver Horace Williams for the second time and robbed him of the Wells Fargo express box and mail pouches. His profits from the express amounted to exactly thirty-five cents.

No. 26. November 23, 1882. Again in Sonoma County between Lakeport and Cloverdale, on the Squaw Creek Toll road at Geyser Road, five miles out of Cloverdale. Driver Dick Crawford handed over the Wells Fargo express box containing $475 and several sacks of mail.

No. 27. April 12, 1883. Sonoma County on the Lakeport-Cloverdale Road. At almost the same point at which his earlier robberies occurred, some five miles out of Cloverdale, Bart stopped the stage driven by Bill Connibeck and relieved him of the Wells Fargo express box and mail sacks. From the express box he realized only $32.50.

No. 28. June 23, 1883. Amador County on the Jackson-Ione Road, four miles west of Jackson, Bart's last successful robbery occurred when he forced driver Clint Radcliffe to hand over two express boxes and several mail sacks. The take from the express boxes was set at $750.

No. 29. November 3, 1883. At the top of Calaveras County's Funk Hill on the Sonora-Milton Road, in exactly the same spot where on July 26, 1875, Bart committed his first stage robbery. This was Black Bart's final brush with the law and many gold country historians list it as a robbery attempt rather than an actual robbery, since not only was it an unsuccessful holdup, but he was wounded and evidence which he abandoned at the scene resulted, a few days later, in his arrest.

NOTES

CHAPTER 1

1. Ron Scofield, Fiddletown, CA. wagon and coach builder: "Mud wagons were somewhat smaller and lighter than the Concord stage, better adapted to mountain travel and required only four horses, rather than six horses to pull them. They acquired the name mud wagon because they had wider tires than the Concord and pulled better in mud and sand. A major builder of mud wagons was the Henderson Coach Works of Stockton California."
2. Robbery statistics: James Hume, Jonathan Thacker, *Robbers Record of 1885*. Published by Wells Fargo.
3. Robbery account: *Calaveras Chronicle*, July 31, 1875.
4. The telegraph line between Copperopolis and San Andreas had been put into service in 1865. At that time Copperopolis was among the nations leading copper producers.
5. *Calaveras Chronicle*, July 31 1875. There is no evidence except the hearsay of excited passengers that the bandit also carried a rifle.
6. Joseph Henry Jackson, *Bad Company*
7. From Wells Fargo & Company reward poster.
8. Jackson, *Bad Company*
9. Richard Dillon, *Wells Fargo Detective*, pg. 168

CHAPTER 2

1. Internal thefts were reported in the *San Francisco Weekly Recorder*, September 26, 1866 and discussed in Richard Dillon's *Wells Fargo Detective*, pgs. 132-133.
2. *Ghost Towns and Mining Camps*, Remi Nadeau. pg. 58
3. *Gold Rush Country* Lane Books pg. 86. *San Andreas Independent*, September 24, 1856.
4. Robert Chandler, "Wells Fargo Never Forgets," NOLO Publications Vol 11, Nos. 3 & 4.
5. Chandler, "Wells Fargo Never Forgets."
6. Unpublished notes of Blanche S. Cook, Auburn, CA. from her interviews with gold country old-timers. The late Mrs. Cook was an *Auburn Journal* correspondent.
7. Robert Chandler, Wells Fargo Company historian in speech to Calaveras County Historical Society.
8. Jackson, *Bad Company*, pg. 125
9. Dillon, *Wells Fargo Detective*, pg. 173

CHAPTER 3

1. *Weekly Shasta Courier*
2. James K. Woodworth and William C. Wilson, *River of Gold*, pg. 7
3. Richard Dillan, *Wells Fargo Detective*, pgs. 173, 183
4. Ibid., pg. 185
5. *San Francisco Call*, November 16-21, 1883
6. Robert J. Chandler, *Wells Fargo Never Forgets*, Nolo Publications Vol. II, Nos. 3-3.
7. *Marysville Daily Appeal*.

CHAPTER 4

1. *San Francisco Examiner*, December 3, 1888.
2. *San Francisco Call*.
3. *Sacramento Union*, Author's 1953 interview with retired 83-year-old freight teamster Ben Green, Foresthill, CA.
4. Dillon, *Wells Fargo Detective*, pgs. 131-132.
5. Lucius Beebee and Charles Clegg, *U.S. West, The Saga of Wells Fargo*, pg. 51

CHAPTER 5

1. *Calaveras Chronicle*, November 9, 1883.
2. Reason B. McConnell's account of November 3, 1883 robbery as given to Copperopolis Wells Fargo Agent J. M. Pike.
3. As told in later years by members of the Rolleri family living in Calaveras County. Also, as told by the late Calaveras County historian and author Coke Wood. *Calaveras Weekly Citizen*, November 17, 1883.
4. Jackson, *Bad Company*, pgs. 168-169.

5. Ibid., pg. 175. *Calaveras Weekly Citizen*, November 17, 1883
CHAPTER 6
1. Dillon, *Wells Fargo Detective*, pgs. 177-178.
2. *San Francisco Chronicle, San Francisco Examiner*, December, 1883.
3. Jackson, *Bad Company*, pgs. 155-159. *San Francisco Call*, November 15-16, 1883. *Calaveras Weekly Citizen*, November 17, 1883.
4. *Calaveras Weekly Citizen*, November 17, 1883.
5. Jackson, *Bad Company*, pg.164.
6. *San Francisco Chronicle, San Francisco Examiner*, November, December 1883.
7. *Calaveras Weekly Citizen*, November 24, 1883.
CHAPTER 7
1. Dillon, *Wells Fargo Detective*. Charles Upton, *Pioneers of El Dorado County*. *Sacramento Union*, July 2 1864 through mid July.
2. Notes on Calaveras County Sheriff Ben Thorn, courtesy of former Calaveras County Undersheriff Fred Kern.
3. John Boessenecker, *Badge and Buckshot*, pgs. 70-77.
4. *San Francisco Chronicle, San Francisco Examiner*, June 16, 1893 and subsequent stories.
5. Melvin Ware, "Mike Tovey Rode Shotgun for Twenty Years," *Frontier Times*, June-July, 1978.
6. Dillon, *Wells Fargo Detective*, pgs. 269-277. *San Francisco Chronicle, San Francisco Call*, October 25-27, 1893.
7. *Calaveras Weekly Citizen*, May 25, 1894.
CHAPTER 8
1. Calaveras County Superior Court Records, Calaveras Archives.
2. *San Francisco Call*, November 16, 1883. *San Francisco Examiner*, November 4, 1883.
3. Related by members of the Rolleri family. (The engraved silver nameplate that was attached to the rifle stock has been placed in the Calaveras County Archives by the Richard Rolleri family of Angles Camp, CA.
4. Wells Fargo records.
5. The *Stockton Daily Independent, The Calaveras Prospect*, May 2, 1903.
6. *San Francisco Chronicle, San Francisco Examiner*, January 22-23, 1888.
CHAPTER 9
1. Hume and Thacker, *Robbers Record of 1885*.
2. *San Francisco Chronicle*, January 22, 1888.
3. Dillon, *Wells Fargo Detective*, pg. 190.
4. *Stockton Independent*, January 3, 1888.
5. *San Francisco Examiner*, January 30, 1888. Interview with James Hume.
6. Author's interview with John Ross.
7. Murphys Hotel register.
CHAPTER 10
1. Pony Express, Sonora, CA., November-December, 1975.
2. *San Francisco Chronicle*, November 16, 1888.
3. Although the story was picked up by numerous newspapers and has since been quoted in numerous books and publications, there is no indication as to its original source. Each user has credited some other unnamed publication with having first used it.
4. *San Francisco Chronicle*, December 6. 1888.
CHAPTER 11
1. *San Francisco Examiner*, December 11, 1888.
2. Jackson, *Bad Company*, pgs. 201, 202. Beebee and Clegg, *U.S. West*, pg. 188.
3. Dillon, *Wells Fargo Detective*, pg. 206
4. Jos. Harkenson, "Tales of Old Nevada." No exact date is included in the story. *True Magazine* in the middle 1960's also carried a story on Black Bart which included the story of the Geiger Grade robbery attempt and fatal shooting of the bandit.

BIBLIOGRAPHY

BOOKS
Beebee, Lucius, and Charles Clegg. *U.S. West, Saga of Wells Fargo.* E.P. Dutton, New York, 1949.
Boessenecker, John. *Badge and Buckshot.* University of Oklahoma Press, Norman, 1988.
Buckbee, Edna Bryan. *Saga of Tuolumne County.* Press of the Pioneers, 1935.
Chapel, Charles Edward. *Guns of the Old West.* Coward-McCann, New York, 1961.
DeMaria, John and Mildred. *Stories from the Mother Lode.* Western Printing, 1969.
Dillon, Richard. *Humbugs and Heroes.* Doubleday, New York, 1949.
Dillon, Richard. *Wells Fargo Detective.* Coward-McCann, New York, 1969.
Gold Rush Country. Lane Books, Menlo Park CA.
Hanley, Mike with Omer Stamford. *Sagebrush and Axlegrease.* Shorp Printing, 1976.
History of Tuolumne County. B.F. Alley Co., 1882
Hungerford, Edward. *Wells Fargo, Advancing the American Frontier.* Random House, New York, 1949.
Hume, James B. and Jonathan Thacker. *Robbers Record of 1885.*
Jackson, Joseph Henry. *Bad Company.* Harcourt, Brace & Co., New York, 1949.
Keller, John. *The Mendocino Outlaws.* Mendocino County Historical Society, 1974.
McLeod, Norman. *Gold, Guns & Gallantry.* Goldridge Press, 1987.
Nadeau, Remi. *Ghost Towns and Mining Camps of California.* Ward Richie Press, 1949.
Stone, Rhoda and Charles. *The Tools Are on the Bar.* Columbine Press, 1991.
Upton, Charles. *Pioneers of El Dorado County.* 1906.
Wood, Coke. *Tales of Old Calaveras.* 1949.

NEWSPAPERS
Amador Dispatch
Amador Ledger
Calaveras Chronicle
Calaveras Prospect
Calaveras Weekly Citizen
Grass Valley Union
Marysville Daily Appeal
Mendocino Beacon
Mendocino Democrat
Oakdale Wheat Grower
Oroville Mercury
Placer Herald

Red Bluff Sentinel
Sacramento Bee
Sacramento Union
San Francisco Call
San Francisco Chronicle
San Francisco Examiner
Sonoma Democrat
Sonora Union Democrat
Stockton Daily Independent
Stockton Record
Trinity Journal
Ukiah Daily Journal
Weekly Shasta Courier

PERIODICALS AND OTHER PUBLICATIONS

American West, "Train Robbery," Richard Patterson, March-April 1977.
Frontier Times, "Mike Tovey Rode Shotgun for Twenty Years," Melvin H. Ware, June-July 1978.
Las Calaveras, quarterly publication of Calaveras County Historical Society.
NOLA Publications, National Association and Center for Outlaw and Lawman History, "Wells Fargo Never Forgets," Robert J. Chandler, Winter-Spring, 1987.
Wells Fargo & Company: Wells Fargo Since 1852.

OTHER SOURCES

Oral History: related by the late Blanche S. Cook, Auburn, California, from her 1925 interview with William (Billy) Foster, who sheltered Black Bart in his Yuba River cabin in December 1881.

Oral History: related by the late Harry Webb, Tujunga, California, concerning fatal shooting by Wells Fargo messenger of stage coach robber on Geiger Grade. Webb spent a lifetime in Nevada. He was a cowboy, trapper, Nevada historian and writer.

Lorrayne Kennedy, San Andreas, California. Director, Calaveras County Archives.

Larry Cenotto, Jackson, California. Author, Mother Lode historian, and Amador County Archives director.

Ron Scofield, Fiddletown, California. Artist, western transportation historian and professional builder and restorer of wagons, buggies and stage coaches. Provided much of the information on stage and freight wagon travel and drivers.

INDEX

A

Abbott, Downing and
  Company 59
Adams, A.C. 6
Adams Company 21
Adkinson, J. T. 29, 32
Alameda County 72, 80
Alturas, CA 19, 27, 36
Amador County 23, 53, 103,
  104, 114, 117
American Gold News 128
American River 40, 42, 50, 95
Angels Camp, CA 58, 68, 80,
  84
Arcata, CA 13
Arizona 25
Auburn, CA 20, 21, 23, 26, 53,
  152
Aull, Charles 56, 125, 137
Aurora, CA 102, 156
Ayer, Joseph William 45

B

Baker, Jim 61
Baldwin, E. S. "Lucky" 15, 149
Barry, Dan 12
Barter, Richard "Rattlesnake
  Dick" 21
Bartlet Springs 14
Bass Hill 19, 35
Battle of Arkansas Post 42
Bear Mountain 69, 71
Beebee, Lucius 147
Beiber, CA 132
Bell, Tom 21
Berry Creek Sawmill 11
Bierce, Ambrose 109
Bigelow, Hattie 19
Blair, Eugene 24
Bodie, CA 100, 102, 103
Bojorques, Narcisco 73
Boles, David 42
Boles, Mary 42, 118, 123, 131,
  142, 148
Brady, Jack 150
Brewster, Lewis 35
Brewster, S. T. 18
Brown, Big Sam 98
Brown, Mitchell 22
Browning, Barry 22
Buckeye, CA 35
Buckley Saloon 75
Bullion Bend, CA 30, 94
Bunds, Rebecca 65
Burling, Mrs. 122
Butcher Ranch 52
Butte County 42
Butterfield Lines 59

C

Calaveras Chronicle 100, 116
Calaveras County 1, 21, 22, 45,
  49, 53, 67, 72, 79, 89, 95, 98,
  104, 115, 128, 147
Calaveras Enterprise 103
Calaveras Weekly Citizen 89, 106

California 6, 8, 9, 16, 17, 21,
  22, 26, 29, 30, 31, 42, 44, 45,
  71, 73, 77, 92, 94, 95, 96, 97,
  102, 103, 126, 127, 128, 134,
  135, 138, 139, 145, 147, 148,
  151, 152, 155, 156
California Stage Company 59
Camptonville, CA 21, 36
Carson City, NV 94
Carson, E. B. 93
"Case of Summerfield, The"
  88
Centerville, CA 13
Chase, George 29
Chickasaw Bayou 42
Chilean nationals 96, 97, 98
Chinese 94
Chinese Camp 22, 69
Civil War 26, 35, 85
Clarke, Charles 97, 98
Clegg, Charles 147
Clinton, CA 80
Cloverdale, CA 40, 48, 56
Coffey, Daniel 41
Colfax, CA 21, 23
Columbia, CA 93
Comstock Lode 154
Concord, Massachusetts 59
Concord stagecoach 52, 59
Connibeck, Bill 56
Contra Costa County 44
Cool, CA 72
Cooper, Charlie 28
Copperopolis, CA 1, 5, 22, 66,
  110, 128
Cottonwood, CA 6, 7
Coulter, A. H. 100
Covelo, CA 13
Coyote Creek 22
Crawford, Ed 48
Crawford, Mrs. J. G. 68, 84
Cripple Creek, Colorado 148
Cummings, William F. 109
Cunningham, Tom 67, 128,
  145

D

Dallas, Georgia 44
Davis, F. D. 105
Davis, John H. 106
Decatur, Illinois 42
Dechamps, Joe 45, 117
Delaware County, New York
  92
DeMaria, John 50
DeTell, Hugh 94
Dietz Opera House 123
Dillon, Richard 56
Dobbins, CA 36
Dobbin's Ranch 38
Dorsey, Charles 109
Dorsey, Sam 23
Downieville, CA 36, 37, 111,
  132
Duncan Mills, CA 9, 27, 85
Dutch Charlie,
  See: Hartmann, Karl

E

Eagle Creek, CA 29, 32
Echo Creek, CA 94
Eddings, Nort 29
El Dorado County 30, 42, 50,
  72, 93, 95
Eproson, Robert Lee 115
Eureka, CA 134, 136
Evans, William 104
Express Gazette 127

F

Fair, James 15
Ferguson and Biggs'
  California Laundry 75
Ferguson, Phineas 75
Fiddletown, CA 94
Flood, James 15
Folsom Prison 148
Forbestown, CA 18
Ford's Bar Trail 50
foreign miners' tax 99
Foresthill, CA 23, 40, 50, 53,
  72, 152
Forse, Harry 40, 45
Forse, Thomas B. 44
Foster, William "Billy" 26, 39,
  46
Fowler, Alex 13
Fox, Frank 17
Fuller, Fred 108
Funk Hill 1, 2, 6, 7, 24, 58, 62,
  68, 74, 79, 80, 88, 100, 108

G

Garvin, John 143, 145
Geiger Grade 154
Georgetown, CA 23, 50
Georgia 26
Getchell, C. W. 103
Getchell, Clarence 103
Golden West Hotel 149
Goodwin Act 90, 120
Gorton, H. L. 148
Gottschalk, C. V. 89
Grangers Bank 9
Grass Valley, CA 23, 32
Green, Ben 53
Greenwood, CA 23, 72
Grizzly Bear House 52
Grizzly Flat, CA 93

H

Hacket, George 47
Halleck, George 7
Hammett, George 49
Hangtown, See: Placerville
Hannibal, Missouri 118, 123,
  148
Harrington, Alkali Jim 28
Hartmann, Karl 149, 150
Hawk Eye Station 52
Hearst, William Randolph 83,
  119
Helm, George 47

Henderson Coach Company 59
Henry's Hotel 9, 27
Hill Lake, CA 35
Hodges, Thomas J. 91
Hogan, Mike 6
Hopland, CA 41
Hume, James 4, 5, 6, 8, 10, 14, 16, 20, 23, 24, 26, 27, 28, 29, 30, 32, 36, 37, 49, 51, 53, 55, 67, 68, 72, 74, 76, 77, 78, 79, 80, 82, 83, 88, 91, 92, 93, 94, 95, 100, 103, 104, 105, 106, 107, 109, 111, 113, 114, 117, 118, 119, 120, 123, 124, 125, 126, 127, 128, 131, 132, 134, 135, 136, 137, 139, 140, 141, 142, 143, 144, 145, 146, 147, 148, 149, 150, 151, 154, 156
Hume, John 92

I

Idaho 44, 119
Illinois 95
Illinoistown (Colfax) 21
Independence, MO 42
Indiana 30
Interstate 80, CA 21
Ione, CA 50, 53, 57, 101, 102, 114, 116
Iowa Hill, CA 25

J

Jackson, CA 50, 57, 80, 100, 101, 103, 105, 116
Jackson, Fred 24, 58
Jamestown, CA 93
Jenny Lind, CA 100, 115
Johnson, Andy 53
Jones, Bill 41
Jones, W. C. 102, 156

K

Kean, P.H. 89
Kearney Street, San Francisco 41, 87
Kelsey, CA 94
Knight's Ferry, CA 21
Kohler, August 150

L

La Grange County, Indiana 30, 92
Lake Clementine 40
Lake County, CA 14
Lake Tahoe, CA 94
Lakeport, CA 48, 136
Lakeview, Oregon 36
Lance, Joseph A. 40
LaPorte, CA 12, 18, 20, 47, 49, 54
Last Chance Station 28
Little Lake 44
Lodi, CA 22

M

Mackay, John 15
Madera, CA 132
Manhattan, NY 150
Mariposa, CA 20
Mariposa County, CA 98
Market Street, San Francisco 150
Marshall, James 94, 95
Martin, Thoms P. 68, 80, 81
Marysville Appeal 37
Marysville, CA 6, 21, 26, 36, 37, 49, 94, 111
Mason, Joe 32
Masterson, Christopher F. 105
Maupin, Howard "Pike" 98
McClennan, Martin 27
McCollum, Ike 94
McComb, John J. 143
McConnell, Reason 61, 63, 79, 83, 88, 111, 115
McCreary, Mrs. Sydney 31, 32
McLean, Donald 3
McQuade, George 67
Meeks, Anna 99
Mendocino County 13, 16, 40, 58, 135, 143
Merced, CA 132
Meyers Grade, CA 9
Michigan Bluff, CA 23, 40, 72
Miller, Joaquin 109
Millville, CA 19, 20
Milton, CA 1, 4, 5, 22, 26, 45, 56, 65, 69, 72, 83, 86, 115
Minden, NV 98
Miner, Billy 28, 111
Missouri 42
Mitchler, Frank 129
Mitchler Hotel 129
Modesto, CA 132
Mokelumne Hill, CA 20, 22, 73, 95, 115
Mokelumne River 104
Molino, Santiago 98
Montana 44, 119
Moore, James R. 13, 14, 16, 58
Morales, Juan 98
Morse, Harry 72-74, 76, 80, 84, 86, 88, 113, 127
Mother Lode 5, 14, 20, 21, 23, 57, 59, 69, 77, 93, 113, 129
Mountain Gate 52
mud wagon 1, 52, 59
Murieta, Joaquin 73
Murphy, Bob 58
Murphys 22
Murphys Hotel 129, 154

N

Nevada 25, 26, 59, 94, 98, 128, 154, 156
Nevada City, CA 109, 132
Nevada County 6, 32, 56
Nevada House 122, 125, 127, 130
Nevada Stage Company 62
New Oregon, Iowa 44

New York 30, 42, 92, 150
New York Daily Times 154
New York World Telegram 154
North American News 118

O

Oakdale Wheat Grower 26
Oakland, CA 140
Oakwood Theater 123
Olanthe, Kansas 148
Oliphant, James 98
Olive, John 1, 2, 58
Oregon 6, 18, 19, 26, 29, 59
Oroville, CA 11, 12, 18, 36, 47, 54, 85
Oroville Mercury 54
Osgood's Toll House 94
Ottawa, IL 95

P

Pacific Express Company 22
Pacific House 95
Palace Hotel, San Francisco 41
Palace Hotel, Visalia 132, 149
Paskenta, Tehama County 29
Patterson Mine 62, 69, 86
Paul, Bob 98
Payne, Ed 19, 20
Pike, J. M. 4
Pike's New York Restaurant and Bakery 41, 87
Pilot Rock 8
Placer County 50, 72, 152
Placerville, CA 30, 93, 95
Plantation, CA 9
Plattsburg, New York 95
Plumas County 12, 18, 26, 29, 32, 46
Podesta, Evelyn Wells 147
Podesto, Pete 116
Point Arena, CA 9, 27, 85
Pollock Pines, CA 31
Pool Station 52
Potter Valley 31
Potter Valley Road 13

Q

Quadlin, Dave 18
Quincy, CA 11, 12, 54, 85

R

Radcliffe, Clint 57, 101
Raggio, Babe 103
Ratovich, Mitchell 22
Red Bluff, CA 21, 103
Redding, CA 9, 18, 19, 27, 28, 29, 32, 33, 35, 47, 132
Redwood Valley 32
Reed, James 32
Reno, NV 71, 154, 155
Requa, Henry 62, 66
Reynolds Ferry 1
Reynolds Ferry Hotel 61, 69, 85
Reynolds Ferry Road 1
Rhodes, William H. 88

INDEX

Rich, Dr. 108
Rich Gulch diggings 95
Robber's Rock 12
Robertson, Alec 41
Rodesino, Johanna 103
Rogers, John 94
Rolleri, James Jr. 61, 65, 79, 111, 112
Rolleri, Olivia Antonini 61, 66
Rooks, Frank 104, 106
Rooks, Lou 104, 105
Roseburg, Oregon 6, 8, 18, 29, 32, 34
Ross, Aaron 24
Ross, John 128
Round Mountain 19, 36
Rowell, Leonard F. 89
Ruiz, Ramon 22
Russian River 9
Rust, Richard 104

S

Sacramento, CA 25, 57, 71
Sacramento Union 88
Saint Joseph, MO 42, 93
Salt Lake City, UT 44
San Andreas, CA 4, 28, 69, 82, 84, 88, 99, 100
San Antone Camp 95, 97, 98
San Antonio Creek 95
San Antonio Township 98
San Francisco, CA 8, 10, 14, 15, 35, 36, 40, 41, 55, 56, 59, 71, 72, 74, 76, 105, 122, 125, 127, 134, 149, 150
San Francisco Chronicle 82, 100, 105, 109, 118, 122, 125, 137, 141
San Francisco Examiner 82, 105, 109, 119, 122, 136, 141, 143
San Francisco Morning Call 82, 105, 117
San Joaquin County 67, 80, 83, 117, 128, 145
San Joaquin Valley, CA 80
San Juan, CA 6, 26, 39
San Quentin Prison 17, 21, 89, 98, 108, 109, 118, 120, 123, 137, 143
Savage, Antone 22
Scannell, David 41
Schwoerer, Rose 129, 154
Scotch Tom 94
Scott, W. W. 103
Shady Creek 32
Shallenberger, W. M. 102
Sharp, Milton 102, 103, 111
Sharpe, George 36, 38
Shasta County 8, 20, 28, 29, 32, 42
Sheep Ranch Mine 103
Sheridan, Jim 53
Sherman, Charlie 55
Sherman, General Geo. S. 26
Shine, John 1, 2, 3, 4, 63, 100
Shortridge, Elisha 32
Sierra County 154
Sierra Nevada 21

Silver Bow, Montana 118
Sinclair, Walter 94
Siskiyou County 8
Sixth Street, San Francisco 122
Smartsville, CA 6, 39
Smith, J. A. 147
Smith, Sam 56
Smithson, James 19
Sonora, CA 1, 5, 21, 22, 45, 56, 61, 62, 86, 128
Sonora Union Democrat 89, 110
Soto, Juan 73
Southern Pacific 71, 150
Spagnoli, Divol B. 105
Stanford, Leland 15
Stanislaus River 21, 61
Stanislaus River Canyon 1
Staples, Joe 94
State Highway 128, CA 9
Stockton 22, 28, 59, 67, 73, 80, 82, 83, 99, 104, 117
Stone, Appleton W. 76, 78, 80, 84, 86
Storey County, NV 155
Strawberry, CA 47
Sullaway, John 34
Sutro, Adolph 15
Sutter Creek, CA 57
Sutter's Mill 94
Swain, C. A. 102
Sylvester, "Doc" 69, 84

T

T. S. Fiske, Co. 25
Tehama County 29, 103
Tejada, Jesus 73
Tevis, Lloyd 15
Thacker, Jonathan 30, 31, 80, 84, 103, 104, 113, 148, 156
Thomas Ware 71
Thorn, Benjamin 4, 5, 49, 51, 55, 67, 80, 81, 86, 88, 91, 95, 97, 98, 99, 100, 103, 104, 108, 120, 127, 145
Thorn Mansion 99
Todds Valley 23, 40, 50, 72
Tovey, Mike 24, 57, 100, 102, 103, 156
Trinity County 36, 42
Truckee, CA 78
Tuolumne County 42, 67, 72, 80, 93, 117
Tuolumne Independent 26
Tuttletown, CA 62, 69, 86

U

U.S. West, the Saga of Wells Fargo 147
Ukiah 12, 13, 17, 32, 40, 41, 44, 134, 136
Utah 44

V

Valentine, John J. 8, 14, 23, 72

Vallecito 22
Valley Springs 71
Van Eaton, John 94
Van Sickle, Henry 98
Vann, George 136
Verdi, NV 127
Virginia City, NV 102, 154, 155
Visalia, CA 152
Volcano, CA 23

W

Waldin, David 22
Waltrip, Nathan 14
Ware, Thomas C. 75
Washington, D.C 44
Wasp, The 135
Watson, Charlie 94
Weaverville, CA 21, 28, 29, 32
Webb House 15, 42, 71, 76
Wells Fargo & Co. 1, 2, 4, 5, 6, 8, 9, 10, 11, 12, 13, 14, 15, 16, 17, 18, 19, 20, 21, 22, 23, 24, 25, 26, 27, 28, 30, 31, 35, 36, 37, 39, 40, 41, 45, 55, 57, 58, 59, 62, 67, 70, 72, 76, 77, 80, 82, 83, 85, 87, 88, 91, 92, 100, 102, 103, 104, 105, 106, 107, 122, 126, 127, 131, 132, 134, 135, 136, 137, 139, 140, 141, 142, 143, 144, 145, 146, 147, 148, 149, 150, 151, 152, 155, 156
West Sacramento, CA 150
Wheat, Alexander 115
Wheeler, Mrs. Sam 55
Wheeler, Sam 18
Wilkinson, Ash 9
Williams, CA 14
Williams, Horace 28, 35, 47
Williams, Reelfoot 21
Wilson, Fred 117
Wise, Henry 152
Woodland, CA 117
Wright, J. A. 143, 145

Y

Yaqui Gulch 2, 62, 70
Yazoo River 42
Ybarra, Pedro 97
Yeates, James H. 12, 18
Yerba Buena Cemetery 42
Yolo County 117
Yreka, CA 6, 8, 29, 34, 47
Yreka Journal 29
Yreka Union 8
Yuba County 32, 36, 95
Yuba River 21, 26, 39, 95